Sports Finance

Special Issue Editor
Brian P. Soebbing

MDPI • Basel • Beijing • Wuhan • Barcelona • Belgrade

MDPI

Special Issue Editor
Brian P. Soebbing
Louisiana State University
USA

Editorial Office
MDPI
St. Alban-Anlage 66
Basel, Switzerland

This edition is a reprint of the Special Issue published online in the open access journal *International Journal of Financial Studies* (ISSN 2227-7072) from 2013–2015 (available at: http://www.mdpi.com/journal/ijfs/special_issues/sports-finance).

For citation purposes, cite each article independently as indicated on the article page online and as indicated below:

Lastname, F.M.; Lastname, F.M. Article title. *Journal Name* **Year**, *Article number*, page range.

First Editon 2018

ISBN 978-3-03842-871-8 (Pbk)
ISBN 978-3-03842-872-5 (PDF)

Table of Contents

About the Special Issue Editor

Brian P. Soebbing is an Assistant Professor in the Faculty of Kinesiology, Sport, and Recreation at the University of Alberta, Canada. His research focuses on the strategic behavior of sport and recreation organizations and their constituents. Prior to his current position at the University of Alberta, Dr. Soebbing was a faculty member in the School of Kinesiology at Louisiana State Univeristy and in the School of Sport, Tourism, and Hospitality Management at Temple University.

International Journal of
Financial Studies

MDPI

Article

Organizational Mission and Revenue Diversification among Non-profit Sports Clubs

Pamela Wicker *, Svenja Feiler and Christoph Breuer

Department of Sport Economics and Sport Management, German Sport University Cologne, Am Sportpark Muengersdorf 6, Cologne 50933, Germany; s.feiler@dshs-koeln.de (S.F.); breuer@dshs-koeln.de (C.B.)
* Author to whom correspondence should be addressed; p.wicker@dshs-koeln.de;
  Tel.: +49-221-4982-6107; Fax: +49-221-4982-8144.

Received: 2 October 2013; in revised form: 31 October 2013; Accepted: 4 November 2013;
Published: 8 November 2013

Abstract: The beneficial effects of diversified income portfolios are well documented in previous research on non-profit organizations. This study examines how different types of organizational missions affect the level of revenue diversification of organizations in one industry, a question that was neglected in previous research. Based on contingency theory, it is assumed that different missions are associated with different funding sources. Since missions can be complementary or conflicting, specific attention needs to be paid to the combination of missions. The sport sector is chosen as an empirical setting because non-profit sports clubs can have various missions while their overall purpose is promoting sport. Panel data from a nationwide survey of non-profit sports clubs in Germany are used for the analysis. The regression results show that revenue diversification is significantly determined by organizational mission. Historically, typical mission statements like promoting elite sport, tradition, conviviality, non-sport programs, and youth sport have a positive effect on revenue diversification, while clubs with a commercial orientation and a focus on leisure and health sport have more concentrated revenues. The findings have implications for club management in the sense that some missions are associated with higher financial risk and that the combination of missions should be chosen carefully.

Keywords: revenue diversification; income portfolio; organizational mission; contingency theory; non-profit organization; sports club

1. Introduction

The concept of revenue diversification and financial portfolio theory have received increased academic attention in the non-profit sector during the last two decades with Chabotar [1], Chang and Tuckman [2], and Kingma [3] making significant contributions amongst others. The main idea of this theory is that organizations try to diversify their income portfolios to be less susceptible to financial crisis [1] and to increase their financial viability [2]. Previous research has mainly supported the beneficial effects of revenue diversification on the financial situation of non-profit organizations (e.g., [4]), although a few studies refuted those benefits [5,6]. On the positive side, organizations with diversified revenues were less financially vulnerable (e.g., [7–10]), had a lower insolvency risk [11], and less volatile revenues [12].

While the beneficial effects of diversified revenues have been well investigated, only a few studies have examined what types of organizations have more diversified revenues than others. Chang and Tuckman [2] were the first to show that the level of revenue diversification (or concentration in their study) varies depending on the activity of the organization, a finding that was further supported by Kearns [13]. In their comprehensive study, Chang and Tuckman [2] compared organizations operating in 25 different industries and found that revenue concentration was lowest for non-profits concerned with environmental quality and for animal-related organizations, while it was highest in consumer protection and legal aid organizations. The type of activity [2] or mission [13] corresponds to the industry or the sector the organization is operating in. Thus, it is only a broad measure of activity or mission, which does not consider that organizations within one industry can have different missions while having the same overall purpose. Having this in mind, Chang and Tuckman [2] suggested that *"future researchers would do well to focus on the specific activities in which non-profits engage"*.

The purpose of this study is to examine the relationship between different organizational missions and the level of revenue diversification of non-profit organizations within one industry. Building on the Chang and Tuckman [2] study, this study advances the following main research question: How does the organizational mission affect an organization's level of revenue diversification? The sport industry serves as an empirical setting. Non-profit sports clubs are particularly suited to analyze this research question because they have different types of missions [14]. While every club has the overall mission of promoting sport, several *sub*-missions exist. One peculiarity is that those *sub*-missions are not only sport-related such as promoting competitive sport and/or mass sport, but also non-sport related like promoting sociability [14]. Previous research has supported the notion that sports clubs produce heterogeneous products for heterogeneous stakeholders [15–17]. For example, they do not only provide sport programs for their members, they also fulfill several social functions such as integrating youths and immigrants, and teaching youths applied democracy [18]. These functions, which contribute to public welfare and social cohesion, are appreciated by the community and by policy makers and represent one reason why sports clubs receive financial support from the government. Thus, clubs also produce other *products* in addition to sport programs.

The variety of stakeholders may be one reason why sports organizations were found to have more diversified revenues than non-profits in other industries [2,19]. Similar to the general non-profit sector, the beneficial effects of revenue diversification have also been shown in the sport industry. For example, previous research documented that non-profit sports organizations with a diversified income portfolio are in a better financial condition [19], are less financially vulnerable [20], and have less volatile revenues [21], although not all studies could support a positive relationship [22]. However, it has not yet been examined how different types of organizational missions affect the level of revenue diversification, *i.e.*, what types of clubs have more diversified revenues than others. To analyze this question, data from a nationwide panel survey of non-profit sports clubs in Germany are used (n = 45,074). The regression results show that the level of revenue diversification is affected by the organizational mission. The findings have implications for club management.

2. Theoretical Framework and Literature Review

Following Kearns [13], several theories can be advanced that explain an organization's revenue composition. The theoretical streams can be assigned to four main areas including organizational behavior, political science, economics, and strategic management. They provide different perspectives on the factors associated with income portfolios of non-profits. For the present research looking at the influence of organizational mission on revenue diversification only streams from organizational behavior, political sciences, and economics are considered relevant. Strategic management theories such as resource dependence approaches look at the relationship between organizations and the external entities that support those [2] and how those relationships result in external control and power. Their focus is more on the consequences of revenue composition and not on the influencing factors; therefore, strategic management theories are neglected. This study combines the organizational behavior perspective (contingency theory) with the political science and the financial perspective (financial portfolio theory) from economics.

Kearns [13] advances one theoretical approach that he calls the *contingency theory of income diversification* that can be assigned to the literature on organizational behavior. When looking at all the theoretical approaches, Kearns [13] notes that: *"the contingency theory seems to be the most promising and intuitively appealing"*. Yet, it has not been well developed in the context of revenue diversification so far. This is different for other organizational contexts such as organizational structure and leadership (e.g., [23,24]). The contingency theory was developed by Kearns [13] based on the findings of the Chang and Tuckman [2] study—the authors themselves have not developed such a theory in their paper. According to Kearns [13], the main idea of this theory is that an organization's mission determines the concentration (or diversification) of its income sources, an assumption that intuitively fits with the present study.

To provide some context, contingency theory is based on the seminal work of Woodward [25] who argued at the time that several contingencies such as technology and external stakeholders (e.g., government, consumers) influence organizational behavior. Generally speaking, contingency theories have the underlying assumption that there is no optimal way of managing organizations that can be applied to all organizations. In fact, the management of each organization is *contingent* on internal factors (e.g., organizational culture) and external factors (e.g., environment, regulations) that vary among organizations [23]. Consequently, those factors that are potentially variable are called *contingency factors*.

In this study, the focus is on internal contingency factors relating to organizational mission. The theory supports the notion that organizations within one industry cannot be treated equally because they are likely to have different missions that are contingent on various internal and external factors. Different missions may in turn attract different funding sources thus influencing an organization's income portfolio and its level of revenue diversification. The present study seeks to analyze the relationship between organizational mission (as one contingency factor) and revenue diversification. This study tries to enhance the understanding of contingency theory in the context of revenue diversification by applying it to the sports club context.

Following more established theories from political sciences [13]—also referred to as the institutional perspective [2]—an organization is mainly concerned with its legitimacy and acceptance in the community. Legitimacy is also created by the origin of its funding sources. Thus, not only the overall amount of money available to an organization is considered important, but also where the money comes from [13]. This means that organizations pursue funding from recognized sources that increase their social acceptance. Moreover, it is likely that organizations generating funds from recognized institutions will increase their revenues from other institutions because they are considered worth of being funded. This is what has been referred to as the crowd-in effect in previous research, while the opposite effect, *i.e.*, crowd-out effect, must also be considered [26]. Crowd-out and crowd-in effects have been examined both in general non-profit research [27,28] and in sport [29,30].

This theoretical stream has implications for portfolio management in the sense that both the origin of financial resources and the interactions among income sources have to be taken into account. This information is also critical to the present research. Given that an organization's revenue composition is a result of the services it provides [31], organizations should carefully choose their missions (and associated services) and pay attention to the relationships between different types of missions. Organizations' missions may have a complementary or conflicting character—content wise and consequently also financial wise. Missions can be complementary in the sense that funding institutions are likely to support both missions. In the sports club context, for example, missions relating to the promotion of competitive sport and the promotion of youth would be complementary because typically young people take part in competitive sport at the elite level. Thus, potential funding organizations would not see a discrepancy between the two missions. On the contrary, some mission statements could be regarded as conflicting. For example, the promotion of health sport and competitive sport at the same time may not be intuitively appealing to potential resource providers since both mission statements target different groups of people. While younger people are more likely to participate in competitive sport at the elite level, older people are more likely to demand health sport programs [32]. These examples show that the mix of mission statements may have an influence on the income portfolio of non-profit sports clubs.

The idea of managing income portfolios originally stems from financial portfolio theory (e.g., [33]), which is one of the economic theories [13]. This theory has already been applied to non-profit organizations in general [3] and in sport [21]. Originally, portfolio management relates to the composition of the income portfolio in the sense of financial risk and volatility. As stated earlier in this paper, the idea is that organizations diversify their revenues in order to be more financially viable and experience lower revenue volatility. Yet, this study focuses on organizational missions and not directly on financial risk (although it will be shown later in the paper that some missions may be indirectly associated with higher financial risk than others). Therefore, this study is more concerned with different types of missions than with income sources of different risk levels. Nevertheless, attention needs to be paid to the combination of different missions since they may have financial consequences.

3. Method

3.1. Data Source

This research is based on data from the Sport Development Report, a project looking at the situation of sports clubs in Germany. Germany is home to over 91,000 sports clubs that are well spread throughout the country and that provide sporting opportunities to the German population. Out of the approximately 80 million German citizens, 27.7 million are members of sports clubs [34,35]. Within this project, sports clubs are surveyed online every two years. Thus, the project has a panel character. The first wave was conducted in 2005 with another three waves following in 2007, 2009, and 2011. The email addresses for the online survey are provided by the 16 state sports confederations before the start of each wave. From the first to the fourth wave, the number of provided email addresses has increased considerably documenting that more and more clubs are *online*. In 2005, 18,085 valid email addresses were provided, 37,206 in 2007, 58,069 in 2009, and 67,708 in 2011 [15,16,18,36]. The sports clubs receive an invitation email including some information about the purpose of the project, anonymity and privacy of data, and a personalized link to the online questionnaire. This means that respondents can log in and out and that several people can complete the survey, which may be useful given its length and variety of questions. The survey usually starts in fall (with the exception of the first wave where the survey started in spring). The survey period is approximately three months and one or two reminders are sent to the clubs which have not yet responded. Similar to the number of provided email addresses, the response rates have increased during the years (2005: $n = 3,731$; 2007: $n = 13,068$; 2009: $n = 19,345$; and 2011: $n = 21,998$).

Each survey questionnaire consists of a standard set of questions that are similar in every wave (e.g., member statistics, sports offerings, volunteers, finances, organizational problems) and a set of questions addressing specific and current topics in sports club management (e.g., demographic change, doping, changes in the German school system, need of support). For the current study, only data from the first (2005), third (2009), and fourth wave (2011) can be used for the analysis since questions about the organizational mission of clubs were omitted in the second wave in 2007. Consequently, the final sample amounts to $n = 45,074$ sports clubs. Since the sub-samples of each wave are different in size and do not consist of the same clubs (although some clubs participated in more than one wave), the dataset is considered an unbalanced panel consisting of independently pooled cross sections [37]. Pooled samples drawn from the same population are considered favorable for the analysis since "*we can get more precise estimators and test statistics with more power*" [37]. Thus, this unbalanced panel is preferred over a normal cross-sectional dataset covering only one wave. Generally speaking, panel data are relatively rare in sports club research. To the knowledge of the authors, the data from the German Sport Development Report represent the largest panel data in quantitative sports club research.

3.2. Measures and Variables

An overview of the variables used in this study is presented in Table 1. In order to obtain revenue diversification, a concentration measure was calculated first. Revenue concentration is measured with an index (*Herf*) similar to the Herfindahl-Hirschmann Index, a measure which has already been used in previous research [2,7,10,12]. Importantly, the index covers two aspects of revenue concentration, *i.e.*, the number of different income sources and the extent to which revenues are distributed equally or unequally across sources [2]. The index is calculated with the following formula:

$$\text{Herf} = \sum_{i=1}^{n} (r_i / Rev)^2, \ i = 1, \ ..., \ 25, \tag{1}$$

where *N* represents the total number of income sources (25 in this study); r_i the revenue generated from source *i*; and *Rev* the total revenues a club generates in one year. To put it short, *Herf* is obtained by adding the squared proportions of all income sources.

Table 1. Overview of variables.

Variable	Description	Scale
Rev div	Revenue diversification = 1 − *Herf*; 0 = perfect concentration, *i.e.*, club has only one income source; 1 = perfect diversification; *Herf* = sum of the squared proportions of all 25 income sources of sports clubs	Metric
	Organizational mission (from 1 = do not agree at all to 5 = totally agree)	
Elite	Our club promotes competitive sport (elite sport)	Ordinal
Leisure	Our club promotes leisure and mass sport	Ordinal
Health	Our club provides health sport	Ordinal
Cheap	Our club offers a cheap opportunity to play sport	Ordinal
Quality	Our club cares about the quality of the sport programs	Ordinal
Commercial	Our club is geared towards the programs of commercial providers	Ordinal
Tradition	Our club sets value on tradition	Ordinal
Conviviality	Our club sets value on companionship and conviviality	Ordinal
Non-sport	Our club also provides non-sport programs	Ordinal
Youth	Our club is engaged in the promotion of youth	Ordinal
LN Rev/m	Total logged revenues/number of club members	Metric
Members	Total number of members in the club	Metric
Members^2	Members squared	Metric
Sports	Number of sports provided by the club	Metric
Sports^2	Sports squared	Metric
Sport	Type of sport provided by the club (ten most frequent sports: badminton, football, track and field, shooting, swimming, dancing, tennis, table tennis, gymnastics, volleyball; 1 = yes)	Dummy
Year	Year of survey (2005, 2009, or 2011; 1 = yes)	Dummy
State	Federal state (Germany has 16 states; from 1 = Bavaria to 16 = Schleswig-Holstein	Dummy

In the survey, sports clubs were asked to state their revenues in the following 25 different categories: revenues from (1) membership fees; (2) admission fees; (3) donations; (4) subsidies from sport organizations; (5) subsidies from the state; (6) subsidies from the district/community; (7) subsidies from the European Union; (8) subsidies from the friends' association; (9) subsidies from other programs (e.g., employment office); (10) fund management (e.g., interests); (11) self-operated restaurant; (12) sport events (e.g., gate revenues); (13) service fees from members (e.g., facility fees); (14) convivial gatherings (e.g., club parties and festivities); (15) sponsorship: jerseys, equipment; (16) sponsorship: boards; (17) sponsorship: broadcasting rights; (18) sponsorship: advertisements; (19) own business company; (20) course fees; (21) service fees from non-members (e.g., facility fees); (22) service fees from collaborating institutions; (23) rent/lease of own facilities; (24) credits; and (25) other (*i.e.*, sum of all other miscellaneous revenues that could not be assigned to one of the 24 categories). All 25 income sources are used to calculate *Herf*. Since the index (*Herf*) represents a measure for revenue concentration, the final value was subtracted from 1 to capture revenue diversification (*Rev div*):

$$\text{Rev div} = 1 - \text{Herf} \tag{2}$$

Organizational mission was assessed with a closed question. Respondents were asked to state the extent to which the club's board agreed to a list of mission statements using five-point Likert scales (from 1 = do not agree at all to 5 = totally agree). As noted previously, organizational mission was assessed in wave 1, 3, and 4. Out of the list of 19 statements that were assessed in all three waves, 10 statements are selected for the current analysis. Using more items was not considered useful given the redundancy of some items (e.g., several items capture competitive sport or a commercial orientation).

The 10 statements cover the main areas of sports clubs' missions. Their concrete wording in the questionnaire can be seen in Table 1.

The 10 mission statements under investigation can be divided into six sport-related and four non-sport statements. With regard to sport-related statements, promoting competitive sport at the elite level (*Elite*) is one of the core missions of sports clubs historically. Sports clubs have the monopoly for competitive sport in Germany. This means that people who want to take part in league competitions or championships at the district, state, or national level have to be a member of a sports club. Thus, promoting competitive sport is one of the clubs' original missions. Also, clubs promote sport for the masses and ensure the provision of sport programs all over the country. Yet, leisure and mass sport programs (*Leisure*) have less of a competitive character. More recently, some clubs also provide health sport programs (*Health*) as a result of changes in individual demand. Many people are less interested in sport competitions; they want to play sport in order to become or remain fit and healthy. Thus, providing health sport programs can be considered a relatively new mission of clubs. Following Heinemann [38], providing relatively cheap programs (*Cheap*) compared with other providers is one of the core strengths of clubs. One of the reasons for the low membership fees lies in the fact that many clubs receive public subsidies [38]. Given the increasing number of fitness centers with some chains also offering relatively cheap prices, more and more sports clubs are faced with increasing competition from commercial sport providers. One of the strength of commercial providers is the focus on quality, both in terms of facilities and in terms of the qualification of coaches. As a result of increasing competition, some clubs have started *copying* the programs of commercial providers (*Commercial*) and pay more attention to the quality of their sport programs (*Quality*).

Regarding non-sport missions, sports clubs are organizations with a fine tradition and thus set value on tradition (*Tradition*). Since many sports clubs were founded in the late 1890s or at the beginning of the 20th century, they are known for being traditional organizations. Notwithstanding tradition is not only associated with positive aspects since it may also lead to resistance to change [39]. Tradition can be fostered through non-sport programs (*Non-sport*) such as all sorts of social events and festivities where values and social cohesion are fostered. Social events are an integral part of many clubs, particularly of those setting value on companionship and conviviality (*Conviviality*). Previous research has documented the beneficial effects of social events for the functioning of sports clubs [22]. Finally, the promotion of youth (*Youth*) is one of the core areas of sports clubs. Historically, sports clubs are particularly concerned with getting youths off the street and provide them with a location to play sport and to learn values.

Since revenue diversification is not only influenced by organizational mission, this study also controls for other potential influencing factors. Since previous research has shown that organizational size has an impact on the functioning of sports clubs (specifically on production costs and organizational problems) [40], organizational size should be controlled for in the present research. The size measures are *LN Rev/m* which is obtained by dividing total logged revenues by club members, *Members* representing the total number of club members and its squared term (*Members^2*), and *Sports* representing the total number of different sports provided by the club and its squared term (*Sports^2*). The squared terms are included to capture quadratic effects of size in terms of members and sports. These size measures have already been used in previous research on non-profit sports clubs [40].

In addition to organizational size, this study also controls for type of sport, year of the data, and state. Sports clubs in Germany provide more than 60 different sports [35]. For this research, the 10 most frequently stated sports in the survey are selected to see whether there are sports that lead to more concentrated or diversified revenues. Since approximately 40% of the sports clubs in Germany are multi-sports clubs (*i.e.*, they provide more than one type of sport), one dummy is calculated for each sport. The types of sport variables are dummy variables, where 1 indicates that the sport is provided by the club, and 0 otherwise. Since the dataset contains observations from three waves, the year dummies control for the year of the survey. It could be that changes in the revenue composition result from events that happened in the year of the survey. For example, financial crisis or other external events could influence a club's revenues. The study also controls for the state the club is located since there are differences among German states in terms of e.g., financial realities of state government, funding, and regulations that may influence a club's revenue composition.

Since this English article is based on German survey data, possible translation issues need to be considered [41]. While the questionnaire was designed by native German speakers in the German language and the survey was also conducted in the German language, the questions and resulting variables were translated into English for the purpose of this article. Thus, translation issues were not present for the design and conduction of the survey, but may be present for the writing of the article. Following Temple and Young [41], the researcher can serve as the translator or the translation can be performed by an external (professional) translator. While the term revenue diversification is a common term that has already been used in previous research [2], the translation of the organizational mission statements is more challenging because the translator needs to pay attention that the statements maintain their original meaning [42]. Therefore, the translation by the researcher was preferred in this article since the researcher is more experienced regarding the meaning of (mission) statements. The translation of the statement *Our club is geared towards the programs of commercial providers* was the most challenging because it could not be translated directly from the German language. The statement should express that clubs are aware of the types of programs commercial providers offer and tend to imitate or copy the programs of those providers. The challenge was to find one verb for the long explanation provided in the earlier sentence. If a word by word translation had been performed, part of the meaning would have been lost. The translation of the control variables was not considered problematic since these terms are used throughout the literature (e.g., [14,20]).

3.3. Statistical Analysis

Following Kearns [13], an organization's income portfolio is adapted *"to its changing mission and activities"*. Therefore, the use of panel data seems appropriate because they capture changes in organizational missions over time. To obtain panel data, the three datasets from each wave are matched and integrated into one vertical panel dataset. Specific attention was paid to ensuring that all variables used for the analysis were assessed similarly in all waves, and are thus comparable. A similar data cleaning procedure had been undertaken in each wave to ensure the comparability of data. During this procedure, specifically the answers to any open-ended questions were checked for plausibility and content validity. Implausible values were set to missing values. Descriptive statistics are provided to give an overview of the sample structure.

In a second step, regression analyses are performed to answer the main research question of this study (*i.e.*, how does organizational mission affect an organization's level of revenue diversification?). The regression models are of the following general form:

$$\begin{aligned} \text{Rev div} = \beta_0 + \beta_1 \text{Elite} + \beta_2 \text{Leisure} + \beta_3 \text{Health} + \beta_4 \text{Cheap} + \beta_5 \text{Quality} + \beta_6 \text{Commercial} \\ + \beta_7 \text{Tradition} + \beta_8 \text{Conviviality} + \beta_9 \text{Non-sport} + \beta_{10} \text{Youth} + \beta_{11} \text{LN Rev/m} + \beta_{12} \\ \text{Members} + \beta_{13} \text{Members}^2 + \beta_{14} \text{Sports} + \beta_{15} \text{Sports}^2 + \sum_{i=1}^{3} \beta_i \text{Year} + \sum_{i=1}^{16} \beta_i \text{State} + \varepsilon \end{aligned} \quad (3)$$

Altogether, two regression models are estimated. In model 2 the variables *Sports* and *Sports*^{2} are replaced by the type of sport variables to avoid collinearity issues. Importantly, there is no reference category for type of sport since it is not a nominal variable—the 10 dummy variables are included the analysis. When T is small relative to N (which is the case for this study where $T = 3$ and $N = 45{,}074$), time dummies should be included in the models [37]. Therefore, two year dummies (2009, 2011) are included; the reference category for *Year* is 2005. The study also controls for state influences with Bavaria being the reference category for *State*. There should be no collinearity problems in the models since all variance inflation factors (including those of *Members*^{2} and *Sports*^{2}) are below the suggested threshold of 10 [43].

The two models are Ordinary Least Squares (OLS) regressions like in the Chang and Tuckman [2] study. In addition to the OLS estimator, several specifications were tried. Yet, typical panel regression models like random-effects or fixed-effects models could not be estimated because of the unbalanced nature of the panel. There are too many clubs which have only participated in one or two of the three waves. Thus, fixed-effects models cannot be estimated without losing observations. It was also not possible to use clustered standard errors to control for unobserved club heterogeneity. Regression models with robust standard errors are estimated to control for heteroskedasticity [44].

4. Results and Discussion

4.1. Descriptive Statistics

The descriptive statistics are summarized in Table 2. They show that the average level of revenue diversification among German sports clubs is .473. This value is similar to previous research on sports clubs where revenue concentration based on the Herfindahl Index was .518 leading to a diversification value of .482 [22]. A slightly higher value of .525 was obtained in another study on sports clubs using the same measure [21]. Revenue diversification has also been examined for sports governing bodies which represent the sports organizations at the middle layers (e.g., at the community level, district level, state level, and national level) of the pyramid of the German sports system. A similar value of .46 was obtained for sports governing bodies in Germany [19]. The average revenue diversification values from this study and from previous research indicate that non-profit sports organizations in Germany have a medium level of revenue diversification.

Table 2. Descriptive statistics.

	Mean	SD
Rev div	0.473	0.241
Elite	2.80	1.27
Leisure	4.12	1.05
Health	3.07	1.29
Cheap	4.45	0.88
Quality	4.12	0.87
Commercial	2.06	1.01
Tradition	3.60	1.08
Conviviality	4.29	0.83
Non-sport	3.04	1.11
Youth	4.06	1.15
LN Rev/m	0.121	0.155
Members	373.9	1113.9
Members^2	1,380,493.6	85,754,551.0
Sports	3.32	3.95
Sports^2	26.61	73.27
Badminton	0.102	/
Football (soccer)	0.283	/
Track and field	0.136	/
Shooting	0.104	/
Swimming	0.078	/
Dancing	0.094	/
Tennis	0.137	/
Table tennis	0.165	/
Gymnastics	0.307	/
Volleyball	0.167	/

The German values are higher than the value obtained in the Chang and Tuckman [2] study for non-profits in the area of recreation, leisure, or sports in the United States. In their study, they had an average level of revenue concentration of .64 (which is equivalent to a diversification level of .36).

Yet, the values are hardly comparable since there are no organizations in the United States that are equivalent to the European sport club concept.

When comparing the average level of revenue diversification of sports clubs with non-profit organizations in other industries (e.g., [2,12]), it stands out that non-profits in sport tend to have more diversified revenues. One reason could be the measurement of revenues which is relatively detailed in this study using 25 different income sources. This relatively high number of income sources could ultimately lead to higher levels of diversification since *Herf* considers the number of income sources. Yet, this explanation is speculative since details about the number of income sources assessed in the Chang and Tuckman [2] study are not provided. Another explanation could relate to the variety of income sources of sports clubs being a result of heterogeneous stakeholders. As mentioned earlier in this article, sports clubs produce a variety of *products*, not only sport programs, but also non-sport programs like social events. Moreover, they produce other *products* such as applied democracy and integration of multiple population groups that may attract funding from different stakeholders. Following Fischer *et al.* [31], an organization's revenue composition is a result of the products it provides and therefore, the variety of products may lead to a variety of income sources among sports clubs which may in turn lead to more diversified revenues.

Looking at the organizational mission of sports clubs, Table 2 shows that the provision of a cheap opportunity to play sport is most important to clubs on average ($M = 4.46$), followed by setting value on companionship and conviviality ($M = 4.29$), promoting leisure and mass sport, and caring about the quality of sport programs (both $M = 4.12$). The mean values show that both historical and more recent missions are important which may not be compatible with each other. For example, the mission of providing high quality programs is cost-intensive and may be conflicting with providing cheap programs. At the bottom of the mission ranking are promoting competitive sport at the elite level ($M = 2.80$) and being geared towards the programs of commercial providers ($M = 2.06$; Table 2).

The clubs in this sample have on average 374 members and provide 3.3 different sports. German clubs are thus larger in terms of members and sports than clubs in other countries such as the UK [45], Scotland [46], Belgium [47], and Switzerland [17]. The high standard deviation of 1113.9 indicates that German clubs are heterogeneous in size, a finding that is similar to previous research [48]. The most frequently stated sport (30.7%) is gymnastics, which includes all disciplines that are covered by the German Gymnastics Association, the national governing body for gymnastics. These are, for example, apparatus gymnastics, floor exercise, trampoline, and gym wheel. The second most frequently stated sport is football (soccer; 28.3%), followed by volleyball (16.7%), table tennis (16.5%), and tennis (13.7%; Table 2).

4.2. Regression Models

The regression models are presented in Table 3. The results in model 1 show that all organizational missions (with the exception of *Cheap*) have a significant influence on the dependent variable. While the variables *Elite, Tradition, Conviviality, Non-sport*, and *Youth* have a positive effect, *Leisure, Health, Quality*, and *Commercial* have a negative impact on *Rev div*. Thus, sports clubs pursuing those missions they historically stand for have more diversified revenues than clubs having more recent and commercial missions.

Table 3. Summary of regression models for the dependent variable *Rev div* (OLS).

	Model 1		Model 2	
	Coeff.	*t*	*Coeff.*	*t*
Constant	0.384	19.30 ***	0.384	19.76 ***
Elite	0.009	4.94 ***	0.011	5.52 ***
Leisure	−0.014	−6.93 ***	−0.013	−6.41 ***
Health	−0.012	−6.56 ***	−0.008	−4.50 ***
Cheap	0.003	1.26	0.000	0.20
Quality	−0.014	−5.03 ***	−0.008	−2.87 **
Commercial	−0.005	−2.22*	−0.007	−3.26 ***
Tradition	0.004	1.98 *	0.001	0.33
Conviviality	0.007	2.51 *	0.004	1.45
Non-sport	0.009	4.66 ***	0.009	4.75 ***
Youth	0.039	16.83 ***	0.036	15.86 ***
LN Rev/m	−0.330	−10.67 ***	−0.311	−10.41 ***
Members	0.000	3.16 **	0.000	3.73 ***
Members^2	−0.000	−2.48 *	−0.000	−2.93 **
Sports	0.011	6.64 ***	/	/
Sports^2	0.000	−4.89 ***	/	/
Badminton	/	/	−0.023	−3.58 **
Football (soccer)	/	/	0.091	18.73 ***
Track and field	/	/	0.017	2.75 **
Shooting	/	/	0.017	2.60 **
Swimming	/	/	0.009	1.26
Dancing	/	/	−0.030	−4.46 ***
Tennis	/	/	−0.004	−0.67
Table tennis	/	/	0.004	0.85
Gymnastics	/	/	0.018	3.17 **
Volleyball	/	/	−0.036	−6.28 ***
Year Dummies (Ref: 2005)	included		included	
State Dummies (Ref: Bavaria)	included		included	
R^2	0.205		0.229	
F	100.753		92.297	
p	<0.001 ***		<0.001 ***	

Note: Displayed are the unstandardized coefficients; robust standard errors reported [44]; * $p < 0.05$; ** $p < 0.01$; *** $p < 0.001$.

The question is why this is the case. Typically, non-profit organizations having financial difficulties try to increase their commercial activities in order to generate revenues from service fees *etc.* These revenues from commercial activities are used to finance core areas of the organization through cross-subsidization [49]. This phenomenon is also referred to as the *social enterprise movement* [26], a phenomenon which also applies to the non-profit sports club sector [30]. Looking at non-profit sports clubs in this research, some clubs also *imitate* commercial providers in terms of programs (specifically health sport programs) and quality. While such a commercial orientation may increase revenues in some areas (otherwise clubs would not pursue it), it also comes at a price. The results of this study show that those clubs generate a high share of revenues from one source or a few sources, but are not able to attract revenues from a variety of funders. Consequently, clubs pursing a commercial orientation increase their financial risk since organizations with a high level of revenue concentration were found to be more financially vulnerable [4,9,10] and had more volatile revenues [12,21].

The nature of the coefficients of the organizational mission variables in model 1 also indicate that some missions are complementary, while others may be conflicting. Mission statements with the same sign can be considered complementary, *i.e.*, combining those missions seems appropriate since the combination does not *irritate* possible funders. For example, promoting competitive sport at the elite level and promoting youth are complementary missions which both lead to more diversified revenues. Similarly, the missions of setting value on tradition, setting value on companionship and conviviality, and providing non-sport programs go hand in hand in terms of their effect on the clubs' revenue portfolio. As introduced earlier, all three missions belong to what clubs historically stand for. The missions of being geared towards the programs of commercial providers and caring about the quality of sport programs are also complementary, but lead to more concentrated revenues.

Some mission statements are conflicting meaning that their influence on the level of revenue diversification is not of the same nature. For instance, the mission of promoting competitive sport at the elite level seems to be conflicting with promoting leisure and mass sport respectively health sport. While the first mission attracts a variety of revenues from different sources, the latter two lead to more concentrated revenues. Thus, clubs promoting leisure and mass sport as well as health sport increase their financial risk more than do clubs promoting competitive sport. The missions of promoting health sport programs and providing cheap opportunities to play sport represent another conflicting combination of missions. While the first leads to more concentrated revenues, the latter increases revenue diversification (although the effect of *Cheap* is not significant). The nature of effects indicates that those missions are hardly combinable. The same applies to caring about the quality of sport programs and providing a cheap opportunity to play sport. Intuitively, such a combination seems inappropriate since quality programs are typically more cost intensive. Those costs have to be covered somehow. Typically clubs charge service fees for those programs to both members and non-members using the programs. Thus, they increase their commercial revenues, but at the cost of giving up a variety of revenues from other funders. Not surprisingly, the missions of setting value on tradition and being geared towards the programs of commercial providers are conflicting in terms of their influence on the composition of the income portfolio. While the first affects revenue diversification positively, the latter has a negative impact. The findings support that clubs should carefully choose their organizational missions and pay specific attention to the combination of missions.

The results of model 1 also show that the level of revenue diversification is determined by club size. Total logged revenues per member (*LN Rev/m*) have a significant negative impact on the dependent variable. This means that clubs with higher per-capita revenues have more concentrated revenues. Thus, the more financial power clubs have, the more concentrated are their revenues, *i.e.*, clubs rely on only a few, but strong income sources. The size variables *Members* and *Sports* have a significant positive effect on revenue diversification, while their squared terms ($Members^2$, $Sports^2$) negatively impact the dependent variable. The larger clubs get in terms of members and sports, the more diversified are their revenues. Yet, the negative effects of the squared terms show that this relationship is not linear, but quadratic. At some stage, increases in members and sports do not contribute to more diversified revenues anymore—there is a saturation effect.

In model 2 (Table 3), the variables *Sports* and $Sports^2$ are replaced by the 10 sport dummies. The effects of the 10 organizational mission statements under investigation and the size variables are similar supporting the robustness of findings. The coefficients on *Tradition* and *Conviviality* still have the same sign, but the effect is not significant anymore. It seems that the sport dummies have overlapped these two effects. Out of the 10 sport dummies in model 2, seven have a significant impact on the dependent variable. Yet, the nature of effects is mixed. While *Football*, *Track and field*, *Shooting*, and *Gymnastics* have a positive effect, *Badminton*, *Dancing*, and *Volleyball* have a negative impact.

The question is why some sports lead to more diversified revenues than other sports. One explanation could be the potential attractiveness of the sport to funders who support the sport. Evidently, clubs providing football, track and field, shooting, or gymnastics attract revenues from more sources than clubs providing badminton, dancing, or volleyball. Intuitively, the positive coefficient on *Football* is not surprising since football clubs are able to generate sponsorship income, even when their best team plays in a relatively low division. Another hint comes from the model itself. It appears that the sport dummies have overlapped the positive *Tradition* and *Conviviality* effects which are not significant anymore. Thus, there must be some sports, such as football, track and field, shooting, and gymnastics that stand for tradition and conviviality, and some sports, like badminton, dancing, and volleyball that stand less for these missions. For this reason, clubs providing programs in specific sports (*i.e.*, football, track and field, shooting, and gymnastics) may be able to generate more diversified revenues than other clubs. The advanced explanation with tradition seems plausible particularly for gymnastic clubs because they were among the first clubs that were founded in Germany (the German *Turnverein*).

5. Conclusions

This study looked at the influence of different organizational missions on the level of revenue diversification among non-profit sports clubs in Germany. Panel data from a survey of German sports clubs are used for the empirical analysis. The results show that the level of revenue diversification differs among sports clubs depending on the type of organizational mission. Clubs with mission statements such as promoting competitive sport at the elite level, setting value on tradition, companionship and conviviality, providing non-sport programs, and promoting youth have more diversified revenues than those pursuing missions like promoting leisure and health sport, caring about the quality of sports programs, and being geared towards commercial providers. Thus, clubs pursuing missions in areas clubs historically stand for are able to generate revenues from more sources than clubs with more recent commercial-like missions. Given that previous research has documented a positive relationship between an organization's level of revenue diversification and financial health (e.g., [12]), pursuing commercial-like missions increases the financial risk of clubs since they make themselves dependent on a few income sources. Consequently, clubs should be aware of the financial consequences of pursuing specific missions.

The findings also indicate that sports clubs should carefully choose their mission portfolio. The nature of effect of mission statements differs supporting the presence of complementary and conflicting missions. While the missions of tradition and non-sport programs go hand in hand in terms of their financial consequences (*i.e.*, they are considered complementary), promoting competitive sport and health sport represent conflicting missions. Thus, similar to the choice of an income portfolio as suggested by financial portfolio theory, sports clubs should carefully select their combination of organizational missions.

This research also showed that sports clubs are a useful research setting for examining the assumptions of contingency theory. In this study, the focus was on internal contingency factors respectively different types of organizational missions. Like in previous research [2,13], the level of revenue diversification was determined by organizational mission. Yet, this study compared organizations within one industry, while mission was equivalent to industry in previous research [2,13]. Thus, this study increases the application area of contingency theory.

This study has some limitations that represent directions for future research. First, this research is limited to three years of panel data. While the sample size is relatively large, the panel is too unbalanced to estimate panel regression models. This may be an avenue that could be pursued in future sports clubs projects. Second, this research is limited to the sports industry and the findings of the current study can only be generalized to the sports sector. They may be applicable to sports clubs in other Western European countries since they were found to have similar financial circumstances despite different policy systems [50]. The generalizability of findings may be extended to comprehensive community sports clubs in Japan that also offer sport and non-sport programs [51] indicating similarities to the Western European sport club system. The results may also inform sport and recreation organizations in Canada that serve a variety of population groups [52]. It would be interesting to examine whether non-profit organizations in other industries also pursue such a variety of missions and how those missions affect revenue diversification.

Acknowledgments: The authors would like to thank the Federal Institute of Sport Sciences (BISp), the German Olympic Sports Confederation (DOSB), and the 16 state sports confederations for supporting the research into sports clubs in Germany (Sport Development Report).

Conflicts of Interest: The authors declare no conflict of interest.

References

1. Chabotar, K.J. Financial ratio analysis comes to nonprofits. *J. High. Educ.* **1989**, *60*, 188–208. [CrossRef]
2. Chang, C.; Tuckman, H. Revenue diversification among non-profits. *Voluntas* **1994**, *5*, 273–290. [CrossRef]
3. Kingma, B. Portfolio theory and nonprofit financial stability. *Nonprof. Volunt. Sect. Q.* **1993**, *22*, 105–120. [CrossRef]
4. Trussel, J.; Greenlee, J. A financial rating system for nonprofit organizations. *Res. Gov. Nonprof. Account.* **2004**, *11*, 105–128.
5. Chikoto, G.L.; Neely, D.G. Building nonprofit financial capacity: The impact of revenue concentration and overhead costs. *Nonprof. Volunt. Sect. Q.* **2013**. [CrossRef]
6. Mayer, J.W.; Wang, H.; Egginton, J.F.; Flint, H.S. The impact of revenue diversification on expected revenue and volatility for nonprofit organizations. *Nonprof. Volunt. Sect. Q.* **2012**. [CrossRef]
7. Chang, C.F.; Tuckman, H.P. Financial vulnerability and attrition as measures of nonprofit performance. *Ann. Public Coop. Econ.* **1991**, *62*, 655–672. [CrossRef]
8. Greenlee, J.S.; Trussel, J.M. Predicting the financial vulnerability of charitable organizations. *Nonprofit Manag. Lead.* **2000**, *11*, 199–210. [CrossRef]
9. Trussel, J.M. Revisiting the prediction of financial vulnerability. *Nonprof. Manag. Lead.* **2002**, *13*, 17–31. [CrossRef]
10. Tuckman, H.P.; Chang, C.F. A methodology for measuring the financial vulnerability of charitable nonprofit organizations. *Nonprofit Volunt. Sect. Quart.* **1991**, *20*, 445–460. [CrossRef]
11. Keating, E.K.; Fischer, M.; Gordon, T.P.; Greenlee, J. Assessing financial vulnerability in the nonprofit sector; working paper No. 27. The Hauser Center for Nonprofit Organizations, Harvard University: Cambridge, MA, USA, 2005; Available online: http://ksgnotes1.harvard.edu/research/wpaper.nsf/rwp/RWP05-05-002/ (accessed on 14 September 2013).
12. Carroll, D.A.; Stater, K.J. Revenue diversification in nonprofit organizations: Does it lead to financial stability? *J. Publ. Adm. Res. Theor.* **2009**, *19*, 947–966. [CrossRef]
13. Kearns, K. Income Portfolios. In *Financing Nonprofits: Putting Theory into Practice*; Young, D.R., Ed.; AltaMira Press: Lanham, MD, USA, 2007; pp. 291–314.
14. Nagel, S. Goals of sports clubs. *Eur. J. Sport Soc.* **2008**, *5*, 121–141.
15. Breuer, C.; Wicker, P. *Sports Development Report 2009/2010. Analysis of the Situation of Sports Clubs in Germany*; Abbreviated Version; Sportverlag Strauß: Cologne, Germany, 2011.
16. Breuer, C.; Feiler, S. *Sports Development Report 2011/2012: Analysis of the Situation of Sports Clubs in Germany*; Abbreviated Version; Sportverlag Strauß: Cologne, Germany, 2013.
17. Lamprecht, M.; Fischer, A.; Stamm, H. *Die Schweizer Sportvereine: Strukturen, Leistungen, Herausforderungen [Sports clubs in Switzerland: Structures, performances, and challenges]*; (in German). Seismo: Zürich, Swizerland, 2012.
18. Breuer, C.; Wicker, P. Sports Clubs in Germany. In *Sport Development Report 2007/2008. Analysis of the Sports Clubs' Situation in Germany*; Abbreviated Version; Breuer, C., Ed.; Sportverlag Strauß: Cologne, Germany, 2009; pp. 5–50.
19. Wicker, P.; Breuer, C. Examining the financial condition of sport governing bodies: The effects of revenue diversification and organizational success factors. *Voluntas* **2013**, in press. [CrossRef]
20. Cordery, C.J.; Sim, D.; Baskerville, R.F. Three models, one goal: Assessing financial vulnerability in New Zealand amateur sports clubs. *Sport Manag. Rev.* **2013**, *16*, 186–199. [CrossRef]
21. Wicker, P.; Longley, N.; Breuer, C. Revenue volatility in German nonprofit sports clubs. *Nonprof. Volunt. Sect. Q.* **2013**. [CrossRef]
22. Wicker, P.; Breuer, C. Understanding the importance of organizational resources to explain organizational problems: Evidence from nonprofit sport clubs in Germany. *Voluntas* **2013**, *24*, 461–484. [CrossRef]
23. Morgan, G. *Images of organization*; Sage Publications: Thousand Oaks, CA, USA, 2007.
24. Thompson, J.D. *Organizations in action*; McGraw Hill: New York, NY, USA, 1967.
25. Woodward, J. *Management and Technology*; Her Majesty's Stationary Office: London, UK, 1958.
26. Young, D. Why Study Nonprofit Finance? In *Financing Nonprofits: Putting Theory into Practice*; Young, D.R., Ed.; AltaMira Press: Lanham, MD, USA, 2007; pp. 3–20.
27. Okten, C.; Weisbrod, B.A. Determinants of donations in private nonprofit markets. *J. Public Econ.* **2000**, *75*, 255–272. [CrossRef]

28. Steinberg, R. Does government spending crowd out donations? *Ann. Public Coop. Econ.* **1991**, *62*, 591–612. [CrossRef]

29. Enjolras, B. The commercialization of voluntary sport organizations in Norway. *Nonprof. Volunt. Sect. Q.* **2002**, *31*, 352–376. [CrossRef]

30. Wicker, P.; Breuer, C.; Hennigs, B. Understanding the interactions among revenue categories using elasticity measures—evidence from a longitudinal sample of non-profit sport clubs in Germany. *Sport Manag. Rev.* **2012**, *15*, 318–329. [CrossRef]

31. Fischer, R.L.; Wilsker, A.; Young, D.R. Exploring the revenue mix of nonprofit organizations: Does it relate to publicness? *Nonprof. Volunt. Sect. Q.* **2011**, *40*, 662–681. [CrossRef]

32. Breuer, C.; Hallmann, K.; Wicker, P. Determinants of sport participation in different sports. *Manag. Leis.* **2011**, *16*, 269–286. [CrossRef]

33. Markowitz, H. Portfolio selection. *J. Financ.* **1952**, *7*, 77–91.

34. It must be considered that people who are members of several sports clubs are counted several times in the member statistics. Thus, the overall number of club members in Germany is likely to be smaller than 27.7 million.

35. DOSB. *Bestandserhebung 2012 [Member statistics 2012].* (in German). 2013. Available online: http://www.dosb.de/fileadmin/sharepoint/Materialien%20%7B82A97D74--24-2687--47-4A29--99-9C16--46-4232BAC7DC73%7D/Bestandserhebung_2012.pdf (accessed on 10 September 2013).

36. Breuer, C.; Haase, A. Methode. In *Sportentwicklungsbericht 2005/2006. Analyse zur Situation der Sportvereine in Deutschland [Sport Development Report 2005/2006. Analysis of the sport clubs' situation in Germany];* (in German). Breuer, C., Ed.; Sport und Buch Strauß: Cologne, Germany, 2009; pp. 641–663.

37. Wooldridge, J.M. *Introductory Econometrics: A Modern Approach,* 5th ed.; South-Western: Mason, OH, USA, 2013.

38. Heinemann, K. *Einführung in die Ökonomie des Sports: Ein Handbuch [Introduction into the economics of sports: a handbook];* (in German). Hofmann: Schorndorf, Germany, 1995.

39. Thiel, A.; Mayer, J. Characteristics of voluntary sports clubs management: A sociological perspective. *Eur. Sport Manag. Quart.* **2009**, *9*, 81–98. [CrossRef]

40. Wicker, P.; Breuer, C.; Lamprecht, M.; Fischer, A. Does club size matter? An examination economies of scale, economies of scope, and organizational problems. *J. Sport Manag.* **2013**, in press.

41. Temple, B.; Young, A. Qualitative research and translation dilemmas. *Qual. Res.* **2004**, *4*, 161–178. [CrossRef]

42. Esposito, N. From meaning to meaning: The influence of translation techniques on Non-English focus group research. *Qual. Health Res.* **2001**, *11*, 568–579. [CrossRef]

43. Hair, J.F.; Black, W.; Babin, B. *Multivariate Data Analysis;* Pearson Prentice Hall: Upper Saddle River, NJ, USA, 2006.

44. White, H. A heteroskedasticity-consistent covariance matrix estimator and a direct test for heteroskedasticity. *Econometrica* **1980**, *48*, 817–838. [CrossRef]

45. Taylor, P.; Barrett, D.; Nichols, G. *Survey of Sports Clubs 2009;* CCPR: London, UK, 2009.

46. Allison, M. *Sports Clubs in Scotland;* Sportscotland: Edinburgh, UK, 2001.

47. Scheerder, J.; Vos, S. *Sportclubs in beeld: Basisrapportering over het Vlaamse Sportclub Panel 2009 (VSP09) [Sport clubs at a glance: Basic report of the Flemish sport club panel 2009] (in Flemish) (Sport Policy & Management Report No. 4);* K.U. Leuven/Research unit of Social Kinesiology and Sport Management: Leuven, Belgium, 2010.

48. Emrich, E.; Pitsch, W.; Papathanassiou, V. *Die Sportvereine: Ein Versuch auf empirischer Grundlage [The sports clubs: An attempt on an empirical basis];* (in German). Hofmann: Schorndorf, Germany, 2001.

49. James, E.; Young, D.R. Fee Income and Commercial Ventures. In *Financing Nonprofits: Putting Theory into Practice;* Young, D.R., Ed.; AltaMira Press: Lanham, MD, USA, 2007; pp. 93–119.

50. Vos, S.; Wicker, P.; Breuer, C.; Scheerder, J. Sports policy systems in regulated Rhineland welfare states: Similarities and differences in financial structures of sports clubs. *Int. J. Sport Pol. Polit.* **2013**, *5*, 55–71. [CrossRef]

51. Okayasu, I.; Kawahara, Y.; Nogawa, H. The relationship between community sport clubs and social capital in Japan: A comparative study between the comprehensive community sport clubs and the traditional community sport clubs. *Int. Rev. Sociol. Sport* **2010**, *45*, 163–186. [CrossRef]

52. Gumulka, G.; Barr, C.; Lasby, D.; Brownlee, B. *Understanding the Capacity of Sports and Recreation Organizations*; Imagine Canada: Toronto, ON, Canada, 2005.

International Journal of
Financial Studies

MDPI

Article

How the Economic and Financial Situation of the Community Affects Sport Clubs' Resources: Evidence from Multi-Level Models

Pamela Wicker * and Christoph Breuer

Department of Sport Economics and Sport Management, German Sport University Cologne/Am Sportpark Muengersdorf 6, Cologne 50933, Germany; breuer@dshs-koeln.de
* Author to whom correspondence should be addressed; p.wicker@dshs-koeln.de;
  Tel.: +49-221-4982-6107; Fax: +49-221-4982-8144.

Academic Editor: Brian P. Soebbing
Received: 24 November 2014; Accepted: 9 February 2015;
Published: 13 February 2015

Abstract: In many Western countries, local community sport clubs are important providers of leisure, sport, and social programs. These sport clubs are nonprofit organizations, which operate in an increasingly challenging environment. This study considers a club's direct local environment, *i.e.*, the community the club is located in. The open systems model and the resource dependence represent the theoretical framework. The purpose of this research is to examine the effect of the financial and economic environment in the community on the resource situation of sport clubs (human, infrastructure, and financial resources). The empirical evaluation is undertaken using data from a nationwide survey of non-profit sport clubs in Germany (organizational level; $n = 19{,}345$), which are combined with secondary data on community characteristics (community level; $n = 3153$). Given the hierarchical data structure, multi-level analyses are applied. The results show that volunteer problems are smaller among clubs in communities with high unemployment. Facility and financial problems are greater in large communities. Sport clubs located in communities that could break even were also more likely to break even themselves. The findings show that resource problems are not necessarily due to poor club management, since higher-level (community) factors significantly affect the resource situation of sport clubs too.

Keywords: Environment; community; finance; nonprofit sport club; multi-level analysis; resources

1. Introduction

In many Western countries, local community sport clubs are important providers of leisure, sport, and social programs (e.g., [1–3]). Members join the club and pay a membership fee, which allows them to use all programs of the club. By their legal form, these sport clubs are nonprofit organizations. Recent research shows that these organizations operate in an increasingly challenging environment [4], which may impact their functioning. Following Foster and Meinhard [5] "the environment plays a significant role in the creation and survival of organizations" (p. 44). External influences can relate to the political environment (e.g., changes in policies and public funding), but also to the economic environment [6]. Generally, the research focus has been on the social-political environment and the relationship with the government, and how this affects the behavior, structure, and development of non-profit organizations [7,8]. However, the environment of a non-profit organization includes more than the government and funding relationships [9].

For many non-profits operating at a local level, the community the organization is located in represents the direct environment. Within the community, the economic and financial situation is critical to the organization [6]. Specifically, the labor market situation and resulting income distribution of the population may be critical for membership based non-profit organizations. In communities with high unemployment rates and low income, residents may not have the resources to become a member. Moreover, the labor market situation affects the financial situation of the community's government in the sense that it has high social spending while generating low revenues from income taxes. When the community has financial difficulties, its support of local non-profit organizations in terms of providing financial or infrastructure resources may be limited. However, not much is known about community effects on non-profit resources.

The purpose of this study is to examine the effects of the financial and the economic situation in the community on organizational resources of local non-profit organizations. The research context for this examination is the non-profit sport club sector in Germany. Human, infrastructure, and financial resources are the focus of this research [10]. Although German sport clubs have more members and provide programs in more sports compared with clubs in other countries, they report similar challenges in terms of human, infrastructure, and financial resources [1–3]. The aim of this study is to analyze how external community-related factors influence these resources since intra-organizational factors have already been examined in previous research [11]. In doing so, this study advances the following main research question: How do community factors affect organizational resources of non-profit sport clubs?

When examining the relationship between nonprofits and their environment, it must be considered that this relationship has a multi-level structure [12], which has methodological implications. There are two levels in this study, the community level and the organizational level (sport clubs). These levels are hierarchical in nature, *i.e.*, sport clubs are nested within communities and clubs in the same community share the same community characteristics. This hierarchical structure must be considered in empirical examinations by using multi-level analyses, which represent the appropriate method [13]. Thus, this study contributes to the body of research on the relationship between non-profits and their environment by applying multi-level analyses, which have largely been neglected in non-profit research with a few exceptions (e.g., [14]).

2. Theoretical Framework and Literature Review

2.1. Open Systems Perspective and Resource Dependence Theory

At least two theoretical approaches are relevant to frame the proposed research; the open systems model [15] and the resource dependence theory [16]. Following Scott [15], organizations can be regarded as rational, natural, or open systems. While the first two systems relate more to intra-organizational aspects, the last perspective is critical when examining the relationship between organizational behavior and the external environment. Organizations should be seen as open systems whose performance is the result of interchanges between the organization and its environment [15,17]. Since no organization disposes of all the resources it needs for survival, all organizations are in an exchange with their environment to some extent [15]. Therefore, it is important to understand the context in which the organization operates.

The resource dependence theory (RDT) [16] is rooted in the open systems perspective [15]. Following this theory, organizations seek scarce resources from external stakeholders in the environment [16]. Typically, organizations do not have all the resources they need for their operations; they are incomplete systems [17]. Therefore, they compete for scarce resources in their environment [7]. However, organizations may lose autonomy when external stakeholders exert power and control over the organization as a result of resource dependence [16]. In summary, organizations depend on their environment for acquiring resources, seeking legitimacy, and guaranteeing survival [15]. In the present research, the type of external environment which is considered is the local community; *i.e.*, the municipality where the sport club is located.

Following Oliver [18], this need for external resources is one of the determinants of inter-organizational relationships. This determinant is referred to as necessity—the others are asymmetry, reciprocity, efficiency, stability, and legitimacy. She further states that relationships driven by necessity can be voluntary or mandatory in nature. In the present research context where the community represents the direct environment, the relationships can be considered mandatory. Although a sport club can be founded wherever the founding members wish to, it must be located in a community. Typically, clubs are founded in communities where the founding members live. Thus, the external environment cannot be voluntarily chosen. Yet, it is likely that the perceptions of the mandatory environment are reduced by organizations [19]. For this reason, it is important to sharpen perceptions by examining potential influences of this environment on organizations.

Importantly, the exchange between the organization and its environment is not restricted to resources. In addition to resource inputs from the environment, organizations also try to secure legitimacy and provide outputs to various stakeholders such as members, clients, and the general public [15]. Both aspects—resource inputs and the provision of organizational outputs to various stakeholders including potential members and customers—are critical in the present research.

While the assumed relationships between organizations and their environment within RDT are widely accepted, it was pointed out that the proposed relationships should be tested more rigorously in empirical studies [20]. Although it is not possible to empirically test RDT in its entirety, it was widely analyzed as summarized by Nienhueser [21]. Yet, this summary also indicates that most studies looked at for-profit organizations. This study adds to the body of literature on RDT by examining non-profit sport clubs.

2.2. Research on Nonprofit Organizations and the Environment

The influence of the environment on organizational behavior has been examined to a lesser extent than intra-organizational dimensions [17]. Specifically, the body of research on the effects of community factors is relatively scant. Since non-profits are strongly linked with government authorities, probably more than with any other type of institution [8], the majority of studies looked at the link between the government and the non-profit organization (e.g., [8,22,23]). One reason for the neglect of other external factors could be the availability of adequate data and measures. Oftentimes, the share of government income is used as a measure to proxy government influence [22,24]. One study used the field of activity, the percentage of funding from various sources, and the presence of a state audit requirement as measures for external environmental characteristics [9]. However, these characteristics do not seem to be characteristics of the external environment; instead these are internal characteristics that are influenced by the environment. This example illustrates the methodological difficulties associated with an examination of environmental factors.

In summary, several studies analyzed the relationship between non-profit organizations and the external environment. Nevertheless, some shortcomings can be observed. First, most studies focused on the political environment and specifically the government as an external entity (e.g., [23]). Yet, the economic and financial environment is also important and should not be omitted [6]. Probably due to issues regarding data availability, economic and financial factors have been largely neglected in previous research. Second, most studies were qualitative in nature (e.g., [17,25,26]), while the chosen measures on the community level could be improved in quantitative approaches [9]. Therefore, the body of research would benefit from quantitative studies that apply adequate measures and allow generalizations and predictions. Third, community measures have not been adequately integrated into statistical analyses; they were treated like characteristics on the organizational level [11,27]. As will be seen in the data analysis section, the multi-level analysis is the appropriate statistical test in the case of hierarchical (nested) data. This study attempts to address these shortcomings.

2.3. Community-Level Effects on Organizational Resources of Sport Clubs

This study extends the perspective of previous research and considers the economic and financial environment. Based on the open systems model [15] and the resource dependence theory [16] it is assumed that organizational resources of non-profit sport clubs are affected by the environment. In the next paragraphs, it is explained what community factors may be relevant to organizational resources and how they could potentially affect those resources. Yet, it is difficult to find related studies because research looking at the role of community factors is relatively scarce.

First of all, the size of the community is associated with the resources of sport clubs, specifically human and financial resources. The community size is relevant when looking at organizational outputs such as programs and services that are provided to a variety of external stakeholders (e.g., donors, corporate sponsors, customers participating in sports courses). While club members are *obvious* stakeholders, also customers (non-members), donors, and the wider community such as businesses engaged as sponsors may be interested in the clubs' services. For example, some clubs also offer sport courses for non-members against a service fee [28], while corporate businesses may be interested in showcasing social corporate responsibility by sponsoring and supporting local sport clubs. From the output perspective sport clubs may have more opportunities to provide their services in larger communities, simply because more potential stakeholders are present.

However, it could also be argued that there is more competition for resources in large communities because there are also more clubs and other fundable organizations and, thus, stakeholders have different opportunities to spend their money on. Since environmental resources are often limited, there is competition among organizations for scarce resources [26]. The level of competition increases with an increasing number of competitors and is thus higher in large communities [28]. To successfully compete for scarce resources, organizations may feel more pressure to adapt programs to the preferences of stakeholders in an effort to please more stakeholders [25]. This change in programs may in turn negatively affect potential members and volunteers working for the club.

The few studies analyzing effects of community size showed mixed findings. In a study on Finnish sport clubs, Koski [11] detected a negative correlation between town size and organizational effectiveness: Clubs in larger communities were less effective. A German sport club study [27] revealed that clubs in larger communities had significantly greater financial problems, while the effect of community size on problems related to members and volunteers was not significant. A different German study [28] showed that clubs in larger communities charge higher membership fees, which may be a result of the evident higher competition in large communities. The clubs receive less support from the community and have to charge their members higher fees to compensate for missing income in other areas. The study also showed that problems regarding infrastructure resources (sport facilities) are bigger for clubs in large communities. Given the above evidence, it is assumed that clubs located in large communities experience greater resource problems.

Second, the financial environment is relevant for the sport clubs' resource situation. While the focus of previous research was on the effect of public funding on aspects like program design [25] and organizational autonomy [23], this research looks at the financial situation of the community, which is critical for the support of sport clubs. Research showed that organizational performance is affected by environmental resources [17], specifically financial resources [26]. This also applies to the sport club sector [29].

The community's financial situation is particularly relevant for infrastructure resources (like investments in public sport facilities that can be used by clubs) and for direct financial support. Clubs located in communities with financial difficulties should be less likely to receive public funding, because expenditure on culture and sport are typically cut in case of financial difficulties [30]. The reality is that many German communities have debts and are far away from breaking even at the end of the financial year [31]. The community's financial difficulties are mirrored in the public funds provided to clubs: Only approximately half of the clubs in Germany receive funds from the community [28]. Based on the above explanations, it can be assumed that the better the financial situation of the community, the smaller the resource related problems of sport clubs.

Third, the economic environment affects the resource situation of sport clubs. The focus of this research is on the employment and income situation of the local population. Recent evidence documents that the labor market situation and the resulting income distribution of the population is problematic in many countries [32]. Although the unemployment rate and income disparity are lower in Germany than in other countries [32], there are nevertheless many people who are working full-time, but still receive low wages. In 2010, 23% of the employed people received low wages and therefore needed additional money from the employment office as compensation [33].

The employment and income situation should be important for human, financial, and infrastructure resources of sport clubs. The income situation of the resident population is associated with the community's financial position; the higher the income of the resident population, the higher the revenues the community generates from income taxes. Those revenues should improve the community's financial situation and capacity to financially support clubs and invest in public sport facilities. Thus, economic and financial aspects are interrelated. The relationship between the employment situation and human resources (*i.e.*, volunteers) is probably the topic that has received most academic attention. Andreff [34] conceptualized that there is a possible relationship between unemployment and voluntary work. He recommended that unemployment could be reduced when sport organizations replace voluntary labor by paid labor. Following his idea, high unemployment would lead to volunteer problems because volunteers are replaced by paid staff. However, it is also likely that in this case clubs would not perceive a shortage of volunteers because all tasks are completed.

When examining the relationship between employment and voluntary work, the opportunity costs of time must be considered. Opportunity costs refer to the income people forego by spending time on other activities (e.g., volunteering) rather than work [35]. Following the opportunity cost approach [35], unemployed people have zero opportunity costs (when a *pure* approach is considered) and should be more likely to volunteer because opportunity costs are lower. On the other hand, employed people have higher opportunity costs and are, therefore, expected to be less likely to volunteer. These arguments were supported in previous research documenting a negative relationship between working time and volunteering: individuals working full-time were less likely to volunteer than individuals without employment or those only working part-time [36,37]. However, once the decision to volunteer was positive, full-time work was positively associated with volunteering hours, *i.e.*, individuals working full-time were volunteering more hours [36]. Another study also showed that volunteers are typically highly skilled [38]. Although these findings may look contradictory, Freeman [38] argued that people with high opportunity costs of volunteering carefully reflect their decision to volunteer and only volunteer when asked to do so. Taking the arguments of the opportunity cost approach into account, volunteer problems should be smaller for sport clubs located in communities with high unemployment. The effects of community factors are examined empirically using comprehensive sport club data from Germany.

3. Method

3.1. Data Sources

A combination of primary data (organizational level; sport clubs) and secondary data (community level) is used for this research. Primary data were collected with a nationwide online survey of German non-profit sport clubs in 2009. The clubs' email addresses were provided by the state sports confederations; altogether 63,468 email addresses of a total of approximately 91,000 clubs were made available. All clubs with a valid email address received an invitation email including a personalized link to the online questionnaire that allows logging in and out. After controlling for drop-outs (5399), 58,069 clubs were invited to take part in the survey. The survey was online from October to December 2009 with $n = 19,345$ clubs participating (response rate: 33.3%). The sample is representative for German sport clubs in terms of size and state. Since 2009, the year of the data collection, no major changes were observed in the German sport club system.

In a second step, secondary data on the characteristics of communities were made available. The Federal and Regional Statistical Offices release those data every year, but the included variables are inconsistent. While community size is always included, figures on unemployment and the community's finances (e.g., tax income) are not available in all years. For 2008, most community figures are available. The club survey is part of a wider sport club project where data are collected every two years since 2005 [28]; however, due to the restricted availability of data on the community level, the third wave from 2009 was used for the analysis since the financial and membership data from the club survey refer to the year before the survey (because 2008 is the last completed household year). The secondary data include information about all communities in Germany [39]. They are provided with community codes. Based on the postcode and the club's community name the respective community code was assigned to every club in the primary dataset. Clubs from the same community received the same community code. Altogether, the clubs in the sample are located in $n = 3153$ different communities. The community code is the key variable that links both datasets.

3.2. Measures and Variables

The variables used in this study are summarized in Table 1, the descriptive statistics are provided in Table 2. Human, infrastructure, and financial resources of sport clubs are examined and operationalized with five variables. Four variables capture the perceived severity of organizational problems related to those resources. These are the recruitment and retention of (1) members (P_MEM) and (2) volunteers (P_VOL); (3) the availability of sport facilities (P_FAC); and (4) the financial situation of the club (P_FIN). In sport club research it is common to ask for problems or challenges (e.g., [1–3]). Also, the subjective problem items are not biased by club size like other potential resource measures. The financial resources are enriched with one objective measure capturing whether the club could at least break even at the end of the financial year (BREAKEVEN_O). These five variables serve as the dependent variables in the models.

Independent variables are available on two levels (Table 1). The community level variables are community size (SIZE), which proxies market size and the level of competition for resources as explained in the theoretical part. BREAKEVEN_C captures the financial situation of the community. The profit of the community could have also been used in the analysis; yet, local governments are non-profit organizations and thus a profit measure is not adequate given that they are only required to break even. The economic environment is captured with two variables. The labor market situation is covered with UNEMP, which is obtained by dividing the number of unemployed people by the number of inhabitants in the community. Figures on the potential total work force, which is normally used for the calculation of the unemployment rate, are not available. LN INC_TAX reflects the income situation in the community and is also adjusted for community size. Another opportunity would be to use income from business taxes; however, these variables are highly correlated ($r = 0.989$; $p < 0.001$) causing multicollinearity problems in the models. We decided to use the income tax variable because most communities generate revenue from income taxes, while there are some (particularly smaller) communities, which do not generate revenue from business taxes, as they do not have any corporate businesses. Therefore, the business tax variable is excluded from the analysis.

Int. J. Financial Stud. **2015**, *3*, 31–48

Table 1. Overview of variables.

Variable	Description	Scale
	Dependent variables	
P_MEM	Recruitment/retention of members (1 = *no problem*, 5 = *a very big problem*)	Ordinal
P_VOL	Recruitment/retention of volunteers (1 = *no problem*, 5 = *a very big problem*)	Ordinal
P_FAC	Availability of sport facilities (1 = *no problem*, 5 = *a very big problem*)	Ordinal
P_FIN	Financial situation of the club (1 = *no problem*, 5 = *a very big problem*)	Ordinal
BREAKEVEN_O	Club could at least break even (=total revenues-total expenses $\geq$ 0; 1 = *yes*)	Dummy
	Independent variables: Community level	
SIZE	Community size (=number of inhabitants in the community/1000)	Metric
BREAKEVEN_C	Community could at least break even (=total revenues-total expenses $\geq$ 0; 1 = *yes*)	Dummy
UNEMP	Unemployment (=number of unemployed people/number of inhabitants)	Metric
LN INC_TAX	Logged per capita revenues from income taxes	Metric
	Independent variables: Organizational level	
MEMBERS	Number of members in the club	Metric
VOL_ENG	Share of voluntary engagement in % (=number of core volunteers/number of members $\times$ 100)	Metric
SEC_VOL	Share of secondary volunteers (in %)	Metric
PAID_STAFF	Club has paid staff (1 = *yes*)	Dummy
PUB_FAC	Club uses public sport facilities (1 = *yes*)	Dummy
OWN_FAC	Club possesses its own sport facilities (1 = *yes*)	Dummy
STRATEGY	Our club has a strategy (from 1 = *do not agree at all*, 5 = *totally agree*)	Ordinal

Table 2. Descriptive statistics.

	Mean	SD
Organizational Level		
P_MEM	2.70	1.16
P_VOL	3.14	1.20
P_FAC	2.22	1.36
P_FIN	2.27	1.19
BREAKEVEN_O	0.63	0.48
MEMBERS	394.44	1546.01
VOL_ENG	12.47	23.91
SEC_VOL	23.74	22.21
PAID_STAFF	0.38	0.49
PUB_FAC	0.59	0.49
OWN_FAC	0.55	0.50
STRATEGY	3.56	1.06
Community Level		
SIZE	17.70	50.74
BREAKEVEN_C	0.51	0.50
UNEMP	0.04	0.02
LN INC_TAX	0.00	0.01

On the organizational level, this study controls for the organizational capacity of sport clubs that may also affect resource problems [27]. These are MEMBERS capturing club size, VOL_ENG measuring the share of core volunteers (*i.e.*, those with a formal position), SEC_VOL measuring the share of secondary volunteers (*i.e.*, those who only help sporadically in the club), and PAID_STAFF reflecting whether the club employs paid staff. PUB_FAC captures whether the club uses public sport facilities (that are provided by the community) and OWN_FAC whether the club possesses its own facilities (including a club house). These variables capture the two main types of facilities German sport clubs rely upon. Hiring or leasing facilities from other stakeholders like a private operator, a trust or charity, and a church are less relevant in Germany compared with the UK [3]. Importantly these are not two categories of the same variable. It is likely that some clubs use both public facilities (in Germany, school sport facilities are also owned by the community and are, thus, public facilities) and their own facilities, while there may be other clubs, which do not rely on any type of facility at all (e.g., in road cycling clubs, members may train on the street). STRATEGY is a measure for the club's planning and development capacity, which was found to influence the perceived severity of organizational problems [27]. The independent variables on the organizational level serve as controls and are not the focus of this research.

3.3. Statistical Analysis: The Multi-Level Analysis

For the statistical analysis the hierarchical (or nested) structure of the data must be considered, *i.e.*, sport clubs are nested within communities. Thus, sport clubs located in the same community share the same community-level characteristics. The adequate statistical procedure to analyze hierarchical (nested) data is the multi-level analysis (also referred to as hierarchical linear model; HLM). Following Tabachnick and Fidell [40], "analyzing data organized into hierarchies as if they are all on the same level leads to both interpretational and statistical errors". One of the common errors of interpretation is referred to as the *ecological fallacy*, *i.e.*, applying higher-level results to the lower level [40].

Multi-level analyses require two different datasets because the number of cases differs between the levels. If this is not the case, another misleading interpretation occurs referred to as the *atomistic fallacy*, *i.e.*, lower-level analyses are interpreted at the higher (group) level [41]. Applied to this research, multi-level models allow predictions of club parameters adjusted for community scores and predictions of community scores adjusted for club differences within communities. When higher-level variables are simply included in the lower-level dataset and treated as lower-level variables in the analyses, the degrees of freedom are too high leading to an inflated Type I error [40]. As a result of the nested structure there are fewer cases on the higher level, *i.e.*, several clubs are located in one community. In some communities there is only one club in the data; this is not problematic as long as there are communities with more clubs [42]. The two levels are linked in the analysis with the key variable, community code. The different levels are mirrored in the equations which, consequently, have two-sub-indexes (*i* for organizational level and *j* for community level). In line with Todd *et al.* [43], the initial model in this study is in the form of a general linear model:

$$Y_{ij} = \beta_{0j} + \beta_{1j} XO_{ij} + r_{ij} \tag{1}$$

where Y_{ij} is the outcome of interest for club *i* in community *j*; β_{0j} the intercept for each community; β_{1j} the expected change in the outcome of interest (Y_{ij}) with a one-unit increase in XO_{ij}; and r_{ij} the residual.

Within multi-level analysis, every organizational-level estimate is calculated in separate community-level equations, which are of the following form:

$$\beta_{0j} = \gamma_{00} + \gamma_{01} XC_j + u_{0j} \tag{2}$$

$$\beta_{1j} = \gamma_{10} + \gamma_{11} XC_j + u_{1j} \tag{3}$$

where β_{0j} is the intercept from the organizational-level equation; β_{1j} the slope; XC_j the community-level variable; γ_{00} and γ_{10} the community-level intercepts; γ_{01} and γ_{11} the community-level slopes; and u_{0j}

and u_{1j} the community-level residuals. The community-level Equations (2) and (3) can be substituted into the organizational-level Equation (1) yielding the multi-level model.

Altogether, five multi-level models are estimated. A hierarchical *non-linear* model is run for the dependent dummy variable BREAKEVEN_O, while hierarchical *linear* models are estimated for the organizational problems. The four problem variables are assessed on five-point Likert scales. Following Wittenberg and Cramer [44], an ordinal variable with at least five categories can be treated as a metric variable when the interval distances are similar (which is the case in Likert scales). Bortz [45] states that when these requirements are given, all statistical tests for metric variables can be applied in research practice. All independent variables from Table 1 are entered in the models. Fixed-effects models are preferred because they provide the constant for all groups (communities). Models with robust standard errors are estimated [46]. Other specifications of the multi-level models (e.g., least-squares estimates, models without robust standard errors) were tried, but the results were not materially different.

The analyses are performed using specific multi-level software (HLM 7.1) [47].

Multi-level models require large sample sizes, particularly on the higher level (here: community level). Following Tabachnick and Fidell [40], at least 20 cases should be available on this level. Multi-level analyses were only rarely applied in non-profit research [14,37]. One likely reason for this shortcoming could be the need for many higher level units combined with the lack of available data at that higher level. The present study is based on 3,153 higher-level units and, thus, meets the required sample size [40].

4. Multi-Level Results and Discussion

The results of the multi-level models for resource problems of sport clubs are summarized in Table 3. Since the focus of this study is on community-level effects, no attention is paid to organizational-level factors in the discussion of results, also because they have already been discussed in previous research [27,48]. Regarding human resources, only unemployment has a significant effect on the dependent variable in model 1: The higher the unemployment in the community, the bigger the organizational problem of recruiting and retaining members. This finding can be explained by the costs associated with club participation and the income needed for club membership. Although sport clubs charge relatively low membership fees compared with commercial sport providers like fitness centers [28], income is a positive driver of club membership [49] and unemployed people may not have the financial resources to afford club membership. Consequently, clubs in communities with high unemployment experience problems of recruiting members.

Table 3. Results of the multi-level analyses for organizational problems regarding human and infrastructure resources.

	Model 1: P_MEM		Model 2: P_VOL		Model 3: P_FAC	
	icient	t	Coefficient	t	Coefficient	t
			Community Level			
Constant	3.660791	45.082 ***	3.930460	51.574 ***	2.091705	24.328 ***
SIZE	0.000124	1.015	0.000052	0.658	0.000468	4.289 ***
BREAKEVEN_C	0.002454	0.076	−0.044889	−1.456	−0.000975	−0.029
UNEMP	2.198204	2.416 **	−1.545328	−1.898 *	−1.671486	−1.902 *
LN INC_TAX	0.484344	0.146	6.631643	1.609	−6.880648	−1.748 *
			Organizational Level			
MEMBERS	−0.000036	−1.752 *	−0.000015	−3.641 ***	0.000018	0.581
VOL_ENG	0.003547	1.964 **	−0.001669	−1.837 *	−0.000536	−0.899
SEC_VOL	−0.002985	−3.725 ***	−0.009652	−13.269 ***	−0.004131	−5.248 ***
PAID_STAFF	−0.075336	−2.345 **	0.119982	3.576 ***	0.153535	3.802 ***
PUB_FAC	−0.263328	−7.482 ***	0.146998	4.333 ***	0.741956	18.814 ***
OWN_FAC	−0.024832	−0.746	0.246436	7.586 ***	−0.462229	−11.691 ***
STRATEGY	−0.224910	−14.505 ***	−0.203595	−12.867 ***	0.004163	0.248
$R^2_{comm. level}$	0.058		0.111		0.162	
$R^2_{org. level}$	0.058		0.111		0.162	

$*p < 0.1$; $**p < 0.05$; $***p < 0.01$; displayed are the unstandardized coefficients; robust standard errors reported.

Model 2 shows that unemployment has a significant negative effect on the problem of recruiting and retaining volunteers. Thus, the finding is in accordance with the literature conceptualizing a relationship between unemployment and voluntary work [34]. However, this study is among the first to provide empirical evidence of this relationship using data on the organizational and community level since previous research was limited to the individual level and identified drivers of individual volunteering [36]. The negative effect implies that the higher the unemployment in the community, the smaller are volunteer problems among clubs. This negative effect is in line with the opportunity cost approach suggesting that the opportunity costs of time are lower for unemployed people, which is why those people should be more likely to volunteer [35,38]. Consequently, clubs in communities with high unemployment can mobilize volunteer resources more effectively.

Concerning infrastructure resources, model 3 shows that the problem related to the availability of sport facilities is significantly determined by community size, unemployment, and revenue from income taxes. The larger the community, the bigger are facility problems. This finding is in line with the previous assumption that competition for scarce resources is higher in large communities because of more competitors. The community provides a limited number of facilities for schools that are also used by clubs in the afternoon and evening hours. Since there are typically more clubs in larger communities, the facilities have to be shared by more clubs leading to increased facility problems.

The results also show that problems related to the availability of sport facilities are smaller in communities with high unemployment and high revenues from income taxes. While high unemployment may lead to fewer club memberships and thus fewer people needing facilities, the effect of revenues from income taxes is more associated with the community's or the local government's financial position. Communities that are in a good financial position can afford to invest money in building and maintaining sport facilities which can then be provided to sport clubs, while communities that have financial difficulties spend most of their money on education and child care facilities leaving no money for sport facilities. This situation is not specific to Germany since clubs in other countries also report facility issues [1,3].

Turning to financial resources (Table 4), model 4 reveals that the perceived financial situation of the clubs is worse in large communities with high unemployment. In large communities competition for financial resources from the local government, local businesses, and other stakeholders is higher [28] leaving fewer resources for each club. Also, the potential contribution of individuals is lower when inhabitants are unemployed and, thus, have fewer financial resources at their disposal that can be used for memberships and/or donations.

Table 4. Results of the multi-level analyses for financial resources.

	Model 4: P_FIN		Model 5: BREAK EVEN_O	
	Coefficient	*t*	Coefficient	*t*
		Community Level		
Constant	2.046551	25.576 ***	0.428219	2.288 **
SIZE	0.000255	3.214 ***	−0.000236	−1.084
BREAKEVEN_C	−0.035742	−1.138	0.188273	2.447 **
UNEMP	4.819861	5.454 ***	−2.446856	−1.183
INC_TAX	0.258572	0.068	−4.737284	−0.478
		Organizational Level		
MEMBERS	−0.000014	−1.785 *	0.000039	0.598
VOL_ENG	0.000890	0.841	0.000390	0.293
SEC_VOL	−0.000374	−0.498	0.005485	3.109 ***
PAID_STAFF	0.173759	5.137 ***	−0.051557	−0.631
PUB_FAC	0.031933	0.957	−0.015956	−0.198
OWN_FAC	0.244443	7.152 ***	−0.042499	−0.546
STRATEGY	−0.066732	−4.484 ***	0.019394	0.563
$R^2_{comm.\ level}$	0.057		0.170	
$R^2_{org.\ level}$	0.057		0.216	

$*p < 0.1$; $**p < 0.05$; $*** p < 0.01$; displayed are the unstandardized coefficients; robust standard errors reported.

Model 5 analyses the determinants of whether a club could at least break even (BREAKEVEN_O). The only significant community-level factor is whether the community could at least break even. This means that clubs located in communities with solid finances are also more likely to have solid finances. This significant relationship could be a result of the exchange of financial resources between the local government and the sport club in the sense that a financially healthy government is capable to provide more resources for clubs that are then also financially healthier. However, a different explanation can be advanced, too: The community could serve as a *role model* for clubs, in a positive and negative way. When people running clubs are used to an environment where financial problems are common, they are also more likely to run the club in a way that it has financial problems. More generally speaking, people adopt the characteristics, behavior, and attitudes of people in their environment, a phenomenon that is referred to as *social contagion* [50]. While previous research focused on obesity, smoking, and happiness [50], this phenomenon may also apply to managing financial resources. Altogether, the results showed that not only the mere size of the community is relevant to sport clubs [11,37], but also other community-level factors.

Comparing the community-level effects in Model 4 and Model 5 shows that different variables are significant. Yet, the direction of effects is similar. Recall that negative effects in Model 4 mean that this factor reduces the severity of the problem (which is beneficial), while positive effects in Model 5 indicate that the likelihood of breaking even increases (which is also beneficial). Nevertheless, these differences—although only in the significance of variable—are interesting because both models examine the financial situation. Yet, Model 4 is based on a subjective measure (*i.e.*, the perceived of the problem *financial situation of the club*) and Model 5 on an objective measure (*i.e.*, whether the club could at least break even; calculated based on the reported revenues and expenditures). Previous research showed that both variables are positively correlated [51]. Thus, it is unlikely that clubs tended to over- or underestimate their financial situation in the subjective judgment. Yet, the scale allows a more nuanced judgment, while the breakeven measure is a dummy variable with less variation.

In summary, the regression results reveal that the R^2s on the community level are (almost) as high as on the organizational level indicating that community-level factors are equally important for the resource situation of sport clubs. It also stands out that—despite the large sample size on both levels—some variables have no significant effect and some significant effects are based on relatively low *t*-values (e.g., the effect of UNEMP on P_VOL). The difficulty of observing relationships, which are statistically significant and can, thus, be applied to all clubs may be explained by the heterogeneity of German sport clubs in terms of members and volunteers (as evident by the standard deviations in Table 2). The heterogeneity of clubs together with the cross-sectional character of the sample may also explain the relatively low R^2s—a problem shared by previous research [27].

This study has implications for club management and policy makers. The finding that community factors (as an area of an organization's direct environment) influence organizational resources has implications for the management of non-profit organizations in general and specifically for non-profit sport clubs which are important providers of local leisure and sport programs in many countries (e.g., [1,3]). On the one hand, the findings imply that organizations should not only manage their internal processes, but also take steps to actively engage with their environment [6]. One form of managing the financial environment would be advocacy, which was found to be positively correlated with an organization's government income [22]. While the results support previous research stating that governance is critical to the effectiveness of nonprofit sport organizations [52], they also draw attention to the importance of an organization's environment. Thus, on the other hand, the results indicate that resource problems of sport clubs are not necessarily only due to poor club management, since higher-level effects (here: community factors) significantly affect the resource situation of sport clubs too. In addition to management implications, this study has practical implications for policy makers. The results highlighted that not only the internal, but also the external situation affects the resources of sport clubs and their effective functioning. This has implications for the distribution of public funding: public subsidies may not be effectively directed at sport clubs when the economic and financial situation is critical. Policy makers should ensure to also support the communities because a sound economic and financial environment is important to the functioning of sport clubs. This is particularly relevant in Germany where many communities have serious financial debts [53], which inarguably affect the situation of the local sport clubs.

5. Conclusions

The environment is important for organizational behavior and the resource situation of non-profits. The focus of this study was on the direct environment of organizations, *i.e.*, the community the organization is located in. Community-level effects on the resources of non-profit organizations were examined using the example of non-profit sport clubs in Germany. This study was among the first to integrate the community level into statistical models using multi-level analyses and to consider the economic and financial environment. The results show that not only community size, but also the financial situation of the community, the level of unemployment, and the revenue from income taxes significantly affect club resources. While these results are not unexpected, this study is among the first to provide quantitative evidence of these relationships. Given that resource problems are similar among sport clubs in other countries [2,3] and that the chosen community-level factors are also relevant to communities and clubs in other countries, the findings of this study should be relevant to sport clubs in other countries and non-profit organizations in other industries.

This study has some limitations that represent avenues for future research. First, this study is only based on cross-sectional data. While panel data would have been available on the organizational level, the availability of community-level data is problematic, specifically when consistent measures are needed over time. Given the evident importance of community-level factors and the limited empirical evidence particularly regarding quantitative approaches, this study calls for more research in this area and the application of multi-level analyses. Future research should also examine how the economic and financial situation of the community affects sport clubs in other countries, which—as noted earlier—share similar problems regarding human, infrastructure, and financial resources [1–3]. Another limitation refers to the measures used on the community level. While it would have been interesting to also examine the effects of other financial and economic indicators like debts, gross domestic product, and the number of potential competitors, this study is restricted to the measures that were available. Third, this study only provides evidence that the environment in the form of the community affects the resources of sport clubs. Future research should examine the power relations between the community and sport clubs, which result from resource dependence and external impacts. Fourth, this study is limited to two levels of analysis. Future research may add another layer like the state level or the individual level (*i.e.*, club members) to the multi-level analysis.

Acknowledgments: The authors would like to thank the Federal Institute for Sports Sciences (BISp), the German Olympic Sports Confederation (DOSB), and the 16 federal state sports confederations (LSBs) for supporting the research into sport clubs in Germany (Sport Development Report).

Author Contributions: Christoph Breuer is the head of the project Sport Development Report from which the sport club data (organizational level) were taken. Pamela Wicker conducted the data analysis and wrote the final manuscript.

Conflicts of Interest: The authors declare no conflict of interest.

References

1. Lamprecht, M.; Fischer, A.; Stamm, H.P. *Die Schweizer Sportvereine: Strukturen, Leistungen, Herausforderungen [Sport Clubs in Switzerland: Structure, Performance, and Challenges]*; Seismo: Zurich, Switzerland, 2012.
2. Lasby, D.; Sperling, J. *Understanding the Capacity of Ontario Sports and Recreation Organizations*; Imagine Canada: Toronto, ON, Canada, 2007.
3. Sport Recreation Alliance (SRA). Sports Club Survey 2013. Available online: http://www.sportandrecreation.org.uk/policy/SSC (accessed on 12 December 2013).

4. Enjolras, B. A governance-structure approach to voluntary organizations. *Nonprof. Volunt. Sect. Quart.* **2009**, *38*, 761–783. [CrossRef]
5. Foster, M.K.; Meinhard, A.G. Diversifying revenue sources in Canada. *Nonprofit Manag. Lead.* **2005**, *16*, 43–60. [CrossRef]
6. Scott, W.R. Reflections on a half-century of organizational sociology. *Annu. Rev. Sociol.* **2004**, *30*, 1–21. [CrossRef]
7. Lammers, J.C. The effect of competition on labor management in nonprofit organizations. *Nonprof. Volunt. Sect. Quart.* **1990**, *19*, 171–186. [CrossRef]
8. Neal, R. The importance of the state: Political dimensions of a nonprofit network in Oaxaca, Mexico. *Nonprof. Volunt. Sect. Quart.* **2008**, *37*, 492–511. [CrossRef]
9. Ostrower, F.; Stone, M.M. Moving governance research forward: A contingency-based framework and data application. *Nonprof. Volunt. Sect. Quart.* **2009**, *39*, 901–924. [CrossRef]
10. Wicker, P.; Breuer, C. Scarcity of resources in German non-profit sport clubs. *Sport Manag. Rev.* **2011**, *14*, 188–201. [CrossRef]
11. Koski, P. Organizational effectiveness of Finnish sports clubs. *J. Sport Manag.* **1995**, *9*, 85–95.
12. Stone, M.M.; Sandfort, J.R. Building a policy fields framework to inform research on nonprofit organizations. *Nonprof. Volunt. Sect. Quart.* **2009**, *38*, 1054–1075. [CrossRef]
13. Bryk, A.S.; Raudenbush, S.W. *Hierarchical Linear Models*; Sage Publications: Newbury Park, CA, USA, 1992.
14. Rotolo, T.; Wilson, J. State-level differences in volunteerism in the United States: Research based on demographic, institutional, and cultural macrolevel theories. *Nonprof. Volunt. Sect. Quart.* **2012**, *41*, 452–473. [CrossRef]
15. Scott, W.R. *Organizations. Rational, Natural, and Open Systems*, 5th ed.; Prentice Hall: Upper Saddle River, NJ, USA, 2003.
16. Pfeffer, J.; Salancik, G.R. *The External Control of Organizations: A Resource Dependence Perspective*; Harper and Row: New York, NY, USA, 1978.
17. Cadena-Roa, J.; Luna, M.; Puga, C. Associational performance: The influence of cohesion, decision-making, and the environment. *Voluntas* **2012**, *23*, 993–1013. [CrossRef]
18. Oliver, C. Determinants of interorganizational relationships: integration and future directions. *Acad. Manag. Rev.* **1990**, *15*, 241–265.
19. Whetten, D.A.; Leung, T.K. The instrumental values of interorganizational relations: Antecedents and consequences of linkage formation. *Acad. Manag. J.* **1979**, *22*, 325–344. [CrossRef]
20. Hillman, A.J.; Withers, M.C.; Collins, B.J. Resource dependence theory: A review. *J. Manag.* **2009**, *35*, 1404–1427.
21. Nienhueser, W. Resource dependence theory—How well does it explain behavior of organizations? *Manag. Rev.* **2008**, *19*, 9–32.
22. Moulton, S.; Eckerd, A. Preserving the publicness of the nonprofit sector: Resources, roles, and public values. *Nonprof. Volunt. Sect. Quart.* **2012**, *41*, 656–685. [CrossRef]
23. Verschuere, B.; de Corte, J. The impact of public resource dependence on the autonomy of NPOs in their strategic decision making. *Nonprof. Volunt. Sect. Quart.* **2014**, *43*, 293–313. [CrossRef]
24. Vos, S.; Breesch, D.; Késenne, S.; van Hoecke, J.; Vanreusel, B.; Scheerder, J. Governmental subsidies and coercive isomorphism: Evidence from sports clubs and their resource dependencies. *Eur. J. Sport Soc.* **2011**, *8*, 257–280.
25. Hetling, A.; Botein, H. Positive and negative effects of external influences on program design. *Nonprofit Manag. Lead.* **2010**, *21*, 177–194. [CrossRef]
26. Mulroy, E.A. Community as a factor in implementing interorganizational partnerships. *Nonprofit Manag. Lead.* **2003**, *14*, 47–66. [CrossRef]
27. Wicker, P.; Breuer, C. Understanding the importance of organizational resources to explain organizational problems: Evidence from non-profit sport clubs in Germany. *Voluntas* **2013**, *24*, 461–484. [CrossRef]
28. Breuer, C.; Wicker, P. *Analysis of the Situation of Sports Clubs in Germany*; Sports Development Report 2009/2010; Abbreviated Version; Sportverlag Strauß: Cologne, Germany, 2011.
29. Misener, K.; Harman, A.; Doherty, A. Understanding the local sports council as a mechanism for community sport development. *Manag. Leis.* **2013**, *18*, 300–315. [CrossRef]

30. Wagner, B. Budgetsanierung auf Kosten der Kultur? [Budget Improvement at the Expense of Culture?]. Available online: http://kulturrisse.at/ausgaben/022010/kosmopolitiken/budgetsanierung-auf-kosten-der-kultur (accessed on 11 December 2013).
31. Schlenk, C.T. Der große Schuldengraben [The Big Debt]. Available online: http://www.zeit.de/wirtschaft/2013--09/schulden-statistik-kommunen-oberhausen (accessed on 11 December 2013).
32. Mackintosh, E. Report: Income Inequality Rising in Most Developed Countries. Available online: http://www.washingtonpost.com/blogs/worldviews/wp/2013/05/16/report-income-inequality-rising-in-most-developed-countries/ (accessed on 21 May 2013).
33. Oechsner, T. Jeder vierte Beschäftigte erhält nur Niedriglohn [Every fourth employee only earns a low wage]. Available online: http://www.sueddeutsche.de/wirtschaft/2.220/studie-entfacht-neue-gerechtigkeitsdebatte-jeder-vierte-beschaeftigte-erhaelt-nur-niedriglohn-1.1308326 (accessed on 21 May 2013).
34. Andreff, W. Voluntary work in sport. In *Handbook on the Economics of Sport*; Andreff, W., Szymanski, S., Eds.; Edward Elgar: Cheltenham, UK, 2006; pp. 219–224.
35. Salamon, L.M.; Sokolowski, S.W.; Haddock, M.A. Measuring the economic value of volunteer work globally: Concepts, estimates, and a roadmap to the future. *Ann. Public Coop. Econ.* **2011**, *82*, 217–252.
36. Burgham, M.; Downward, P. Why volunteer, time to volunteer? A case study from swimming. *Manag. Leis.* **2005**, *10*, 79–93.
37. Schlesinger, T.; Nagel, S. Who will volunteer? Analysing individual and structural factors of volunteering in Swiss sports clubs. *Eur. J. Sport Sci.* **2013**, *13*, 707–715.
38. Freeman, R.B. Working for nothing: The supply of volunteer labor. *J. Labor Econ.* **1997**, *15*, S140–S166. [CrossRef]
39. Federal and Regional Statistical Offices (Ed.) *Statistik lokal. Daten für die Gemeinden, kreisfreien Städte und Kreise Deutschlands [Local Statistics. Data of the Communities, Country Boroughs and Districts in Germany]*; Landesamt für Datenverarbeitung und Statistik Nordrhein-Westfalen: Düsseldorf, Germany, 2008.
40. Tabachnick, B.G.; Fidell, L.S. *Using Multivariate Statistics*; Allyn & Bacon: Boston, MA, USA, 2007.
41. Hox, J.J. *Multilevel Analysis*; Lawrence Erlbaum Associates: Mahwah, NJ, USA, 2002.
42. Snijders, T.A.B.; Bosker, R. *Multilevel Analysis: An Introduction to Basic and Advanced Modeling*; Sage: London, UK, 1999.
43. Todd, S.Y.; Crook, T.R.; Barilla, A.G. Hierarchical linear modeling of multilevel data. *J. Sport Manag.* **2005**, *19*, 387–403.
44. Wittenberg, R.; Cramer, H. *Computergestützte Datenanalyse [Computer Assisted Data Analysis]*, 2nd ed.; Lucius & Lucius: Stuttgart, Germany, 1998.
45. Bortz, J. *Statistik für Human- und Sozialwissenschaftler [Statistics for the Human and Social Sciences]*, 6th ed.; Springer: Heidelberg, Germany, 2005.
46. White, H. A heteroskedastic-consistent covariance matrix estimator and a direct test for heteroskedasticity. *Econometrica* **1980**, *48*, 817–838. [CrossRef]
47. Raudenbush, S.; Bryk, A.; Cheong, Y.; Congdon, R.; du Toit, M. *HLM 6: Hierarchical Linear and Nonlinear Modeling*; Scientific Software International, Inc.: Lincolnwood, IL, USA, 2004.
48. Wicker, P.; Breuer, C.; Lamprecht, M.; Fischer, A. Does club size matter? An examination of economies of scale, economies of scope, and organizational problems. *J. Sport Manag.* **2014**, *28*, 266–280.
49. Nagel, M. Die soziale Zusammensetzung der Sportvereinsmitglieder. In *Integrationsleistungen von Sportvereinen als Freiwilligenorganisationen [Integration Achievements of Sport Clubs as Voluntary Organisations]*; Baur, J., Braun, S., Eds.; Meyer & Meyer: Aachen, Germany, 2003; pp. 409–448.
50. Christakis, N.A.; Fowler, J.H. Social contagion theory: Examining dynamic social networks and human behavior. *Stat. Med.* **2013**, *32*, 556–577. [CrossRef] [PubMed]
51. Coates, D.; Wicker, P.; Feiler, S.; Breuer, C. A bivariate probit examination of financial and volunteer problems of non-profit sport clubs. *Int. J. Sport Financ.* **2014**, *9*, 130–148.

Int. J. Financial Stud. **2015**, *3*, 31–48

52. Yeh, C.M.; Taylor, T. Issues of governance in sport organisations: A question of board size, structure and roles. *World Leis. J.* **2008**, *50*, 33–45. [CrossRef]
53. Schäfers, M. Überschuldete Kommunen: Die Krise vor der Haustür [Overindebted Communities: The Crisis in Front of the Entry Door]. Available online: http://www.faz.net/aktuell/wirtschaft/ueberschuldete-kommunen-die-krise-vor-der-haustuer-11619334.html (accessed on 13 January 2015).

International Journal of
Financial Studies

MDPI

Article

The NBA's Maximum Player Salary and the Distribution of Player Rents

Kelly M. Hastings and Frank Stephenson *

Department of Economics, Berry College, Box 5024, Mount Berry, GA 30149, USA;
kelly.hastings@vikings.berry.edu
* Author to whom correspondence should be addressed; efstephenson@berry.edu; Tel.: +1-706-238-7878.

Academic Editor: Brian Soebbing
Received: 10 December 2014; Accepted: 12 March 2015; Published: 25 March 2015

Abstract: The NBA's 1999 Collective Bargaining Agreement (CBA) included provisions capping individual player pay in addition to team payrolls. This study examines the effect the NBA's maximum player salary on player rents by comparing player pay from the 1997–1998 and 2003–2004 seasons while controlling for player productivity and other factors related to player pay. The results indicate a large increase in the pay received by teams' second highest and, to a lesser extent, third highest paid players. We interpret this result as evidence that the adoption of the maximum player salary shifted rents from stars to complementary players. We also show that the 1999 CBA's rookie contract provisions reduced salaries of early career players.

Keywords: NBA; maximum player salary; 1999 collective bargaining agreement; rookie contract

JEL Classification: Z22

They arrived at this specific point after salaries ballooned over the past 15 years—not for superstars, but for complementary players who don't sell tickets, can't carry a franchise, and, in a worst-case scenario, operate as a sunk cost . . .

It's about Andre Iguodala, Emeka Okafor, Elton Brand, Andrei Kirilenko, Tyson Chandler, Larry Hughes, Michael Redd, Corey Maggette and Luol Deng making eight figures a year but being unable to sell tickets, create local buzz or lead a team to anything better than 35 wins.—Bill Simmons (2010) [1]

1. Introduction

A prominent feature of the 1999 Collective Bargaining Agreement (CBA) between National Basketball Association's (NBA) owners and players was the imposition of a maximum player salary. Previously teams re-signing their own free agents had been allowed to pay those any amount that was mutually agreeable to the teams and players regardless of the NBA's salary cap. Likewise, the 1999 CBA reduced the pay going to early-career players subject to so-called rookie contracts. With superstar players no longer able to negotiate unlimited salaries with their teams and rookie contract players receiving less pay, some of the revenues generated by those players were available to be captured by team owners, other players, or other providers of NBA inputs. This paper investigates the possibility that the rents were (at least partially) captured by other players, particularly those referred to by basketball commentator Bill Simmons as "complementary players" in the quotation above [1]. [1] We begin with an overview of the 1999 CBA before turning to our empirical model and results.

2. The 1999 Collective Bargaining Agreement [2]

In their 1983 CBA, the NBA and its players agreed to impose a salary cap on teams with no limit on individual player salaries. However, the cap contained many exceptions, most notably a team's right to re-sign its players even if doing so put it over the salary cap. [3] The combination of unlimited player salaries and teams' ability to re-sign their players led team wage bills to frequently exceed the cap.

Because of escalating player expenses, the NBA won a provision in the 1995 CBA allowing the league to re-open the labor agreement if total player compensation exceeded 51.8% revenue (referred to as "basketball-related income"). After player pay exceeded the 51.8% threshold in the 1997–1998 season, the league exercised its right to re-open the CBA and locked the players out effective 1 July 1998. The lockout lasted longer than six months and caused the 1998–1999 season to be shortened from 82 to 50 games before the league and its players agreed to a new CBA in early 1999.

The 1999 CBA contained many significant changes to the NBA's labor-management environment. The most important features for the purposes of this paper were the CBA's imposition of maximum individual player salaries, reduced pay for players in their first contracts after entering the league (so-called "rookie contracts"), and a new "midlevel" team salary cap exception that would be equal to 108% of the mean salary after a phase-in period during the first years of the CBA. [4] The maximum player salary depends on experience, topping out at the maximum of 35% of the team cap, 105% of the player's previous salary, or $14 million for players with at least 10 years of experience. Although existing player contracts would be "grandfathered" from the maximum player salary provisions, the new caps meant that superstar pay such as Michael Jordan's salary in excess of $30 million would be a thing of the past as these players left the league. Likewise, the new CBA's rookie contract provisions reduced the slot amounts going to rookie players, [5] stopped allowing players to negotiate lucrative contract extensions after only two seasons in the league, and extended team control from three to five years by granting teams an option year for fourth year players and the right of first refusal for fifth-year players. By limiting player pay for stars and for early-career players, the 1999 CBA redistributed rents that would have gone to these players. This paper tests the conjecture that rents were captured, at least in part, by complementary players, such as those listed in Bill Simmons quote [1].

3. Empirical Framework

To assess the possibility that imposing maximum player salaries led to rents for complementary players, this paper compares player salaries from the 1997–1998 and 2003–2004 seasons. The 1997–1998 season was the last full season played under the CBA permitting unlimited payment by teams re-signing their free agents. The 1999 CBA allowed existing contracts to be honored, hence, our choice of a comparison season that comes five years after the new collective bargaining agreement went into

---

[1] That the NBA's 1999 collective bargaining agreement was expected to redistribute rents away from superstars toward other players was explained by Hill and Groothuis [2]. They argue that, consistent with previous research in labor economics, the redistribution of rents can be explained by a median voter model of union membership.

[2] This section is based on [2–4].

[3] Teams' ability to offer their free agent players unlimited pay regardless of salary cap implications was sometimes referred to as the Larry Bird Exception. However, the 1999 Collective Bargaining Agreement still contained provisions, sometimes referred to as "Bird Rules," permitting teams to pay their free agents more than the players could earn by moving to other teams but no longer allowing unlimited player pay. Because of the potential for confusion between the so-called Bird Exception and Bird Rules, this paper does not use those terms.

[4] Other notable provisions included minimum player salaries that escalated with player experience, a luxury tax imposed on teams exceeding the team salary cap, and a salary recovery provision allowing team owners to "clawback" some player pay if aggregate salaries exceed certain basketball-related income thresholds.

[5] Drafted player pay is determined by their "slot" or position taken in the draft.

effect. Most, though perhaps not all, 2003–2004 player salaries should have been negotiated under the new rules promulgated by the 1999 CBA. [6] The analysis focuses on the salary earned by the 250 highest paid players (and ties) in each year, yielding a pooled sample size of 507. Using the 250 highest paid players corresponds roughly to the eight highest paid players per team in each year.

The dependent variable for the analysis, RSAL, is each player's inflation-adjusted salary. The nominal salary data for both years are obtained from Rod Fort's sports data website [8]. [7] The 1997–1998 salaries are then converted to their inflation-adjusted 2003–2004 equivalents using the CPI. Descriptive statistics for RSAL and all explanatory variables are reported in Table 1.

Table 1. Descriptive Statistics.

Variables	Mean	Std. Dev.	Minimum	Maximum
Dependent				
RSAL	4,758,353	4,001,079	37,938,672	37,938,672
Independent				
WS/48	0.099	0.059	−0.186	0.316
PPG	11.11	6.02	0.80	32.10
MIN	1855	879	6	3485
EXPERIENCE	6805	3.660	0	19
HEIGHT	79.301	3.787	63	90
1st	0.114	0.319	0	1
2nd	0.114	0.319	0	1
3rd	0.114	0.319	0	1
4th	0.114	0.319	0	1
ROOKIECONTRACT	0.205	0.404	0	1
DV2003	0.504	0.500	0	1
CTR	0.223	0.417	0	1
PF	0.217	0.413	0	1
SG	0.185	0.389	0	1
PG	0.181	0.386	0	1

To control for player quality, the model includes win shares per forty-eight minutes played (WS/48) which is a measure of the number of wins contributed by a player based on his offensive and defensive performance. These data are obtained from basketball-reference.com where additional details about the calculation of win shares can be found. Since better players should have larger salaries than less talented players, WS/48 should be positively correlated with RSAL. The model also includes minutes played (MIN) during the season; ceteris paribus, players who play more should be more valuable to their teams, resulting in a positive coefficient on MIN. These data are also obtained from basketball-reference.com [9]. In an alternate specification, we use points per game (PPG) instead of win shares because Berri *et al.* [10] find scoring is more strongly related to player salaries than are other measures of performance such as rebounds, steals, and assists.

HEIGHT (in inches) is included in the model because Berri *et al.* [11] implies that taller players should receive a pay premium because of their relative scarcity. Likewise, the model includes EXPERIENCE (in years) and its square (EXPERIENCESQ) to capture the relationship between experience and pay. Including both experience and its square is common in studies of athlete pay because it is expected that players will improve as they gain experience during the early years of their careers before eventually having performance decline because of age or competitive wear-and-tear.

---

[6] In examining contemporaneous salaries, our approach follows that of papers such as [5,6] in ignoring whether players had multi-year contracts and the year in which those contracts were signed. Jenkins [7] points out that using contemporaneous salary and contemporaneous productivity is potentially problematic because actual productivity may not match the anticipated productivity at the time a multi-year contract was signed. In any event, we know of no comprehensive source for data on the length or signing dates of NBA player contracts.

[7] Fort indicates that the salary data were originally published by *USA Today*.

Beyond this usual rationale for including experience and experience squared in the model, it is important to do so because, as noted above, the 1999 CBA adopted both minimum and maximum salaries that increased with experience. [8]

The variables 1st, 2nd, 3rd, and 4th are dummies for the first, second, third, and fourth highest paid players on a given team, respectively. Since the model already includes a measure of player productivity (WS/48), the coefficients on these dummy variables can be thought of as measures of rents captured by the highest paid players on each team. [9] DV2003 is a dummy variable that takes a value of one for all 2003–2004 season observations and a value of zero for all 1997–1998 season observations. A positive correlation between DV2003 and RSAL would indicate that NBA player salaries have increased over time (even after adjusting for inflation). The model also includes four interaction terms (1st * DV2003 *etc.*) between the rank dummies and the 2003–2004 dummy variable. The estimated coefficients on these interaction terms would be interpreted as the change in the rents accruing to the highest, second highest, third highest, and fourth highest paid players, respectively, in 2003–2004 relative to 1997–1998. Our conjecture, as discussed above, is that the 1999 CBA increased the rents accruing to a team's complementary players rather than the highest paid player on each team.

The model also includes a dummy variable ROOKIECONTRACT for players in their first contract after being drafted. Since the 1999 CBA reduced slot amounts for early-career players and extended the duration of team control, the model also includes an interaction term ROOKIECONTRACT * DV2003 to capture any change in rookie pay following the new CBA. Lastly, in some specifications, the model also includes dummy variables for player positions in case there are systematic pay differences across positions. [10] The included variables are dummies for centers (CTR), power forwards (PF), shooting guards (SG), and point guards (PG), with small forwards as the reference category. The player position data were also obtained from basketball-reference.com [9].

4. Estimation Results

Table 2 contains OLS regression results; the parentheses contain t-statistics derived from White-corrected standard errors. The results in columns 1 and 3 use win shares as the measure of player performance while the estimations reported in columns 2 and 4 use points per game. Columns 1 and 2 are estimated without position dummies (center, power forward, *etc.*) while columns 3 and 4 include the position dummies.

---

[8] That mandating pay increase with experience could incentivize teams to substitute less experienced players for more experienced players is supported by Ducking *et al.* [12].

[9] Kendall [13] takes this approach to examining player misbehavior and finds that a player's pay rank on his team has a strong relationship with the number of technical fouls received.

[10] A possible reason for systematic pay differences is the finding by Berri *et al.* [11] that the scarcity of talented tall players (centers or perhaps power forwards) is a source of competitive imbalance in the NBA.

Table 2. Regression Results.

Variable	(1)	(2)	(3)	(4)
WS/48	11,448,470 * (3.53)		11,570,400 * (3.48)	
PPG		205,665 * (4.01)		214,282 * (4.20)
MIN	137.10 (1.10)	−513.83 * (−2.22)	111.92 (0.85)	−522.89 * (−2.31)
EXPERIENCE	448,316 * (4.05)	485,442 * (4.06)	452,496 * (4.09)	482,232 * (4.01)
EXPERIENCESQ	−19,835 * (−2.93)	−19,960 * (−2.65)	−19,818 * (−2.92)	−19,771 * (−2.61)
HEIGHT	45,934 * (1.69)	73,983 * (2.88)	99,898 * (2.17)	74,870 * (1.66)
1st	6,801,080 * (5.95)	5,954,402 * (5.68)	6,795,856 * (5.95)	5,849,532 * (5.54)
2nd	2,663,831 * (8.35)	2,202,278 * (5.71)	2,671,115 * (8.43)	2,169,702 * (5.51)
3rd	1,802,492 * (6.98)	1,662,274 * (6.12)	1,806,055 * (7.21)	1,674,239 * (5.96)
4th	783,174 * (3.37)	931,056 * (3.75)	766,748 * (3.26)	926,015 * (3.65)
ROOKIECONTRACT	572,744 * (1.68)	247,285 (0.74)	613,638 * (1.81)	243,901 (0.73)
DV2003	1,128,398 * (5.73)	1,363,341 * (7.14)	1,127,071 * (5.59)	1,341,995 * (6.92)
1st * DV2003	1,903,845 (1.34)	1,627,122 (1.15)	1,914,272 (1.32)	1,716,194 (1.19)
2nd * DV2003	2,772,432 * (4.40)	2,492,349 * (3.78)	2,771,133 * (4.38)	2,559,076 * (3.88)
3rd * DV2003	1,053,477 * (1.95)	909,989 * (1.69)	1,026,794 * (1.90)	843,480 (1.56)
4th * DV2003	761,291 * (1.77)	405,425 (0.95)	790,390 * (1.85)	416,236 (0.98)
ROOKIECONTRACT * DV2003	−638,726 * (−2.11)	−676,659 * (−2.25)	−690,485 * (−2.26)	−649,338 * (−2.13)
CTR			−299,661 (−0.94)	294,576 (0.92)
%hline PF			−236,912 (−0.81)	52,520 (0.19)
SG			−3131 (−0.01)	−146,332 (−0.38)
PG			398,326 (1.11)	325,586 (0.89)
Constant	−4,502,654 * (−2.05)	−6,755,296 * (−3.18)	−8,731,644 * (−2.33)	−6,985,388 * (−1.91)
R^2	0.672	0.681	0.673	0.683

Notes: Parentheses contain *t*-statistics derived from White-corrected standard errors. * Indicates $p < 0.10$.

As expected, player pay is strongly related to performance whether measured by win shares or points per game. Likewise, the positive coefficient on EXPERIENCE and negative coefficient on EXPERIENCESQ indicates that there are diminishing marginal returns to experience; the maximum effect of experience occurs at about 12 years of experience. An additional inch of height is associated with a salary increase of $45,000–$100,000.

ROOKIECONTRACT has a positive coefficient, though it is statistically significant only in the win share specifications. That early-career players prior to the 1999 CBA were reaping pay of up to $600,000 in excess of their productivity might explain why that labor agreement reduced the pay for players playing under their first contracts. The negative coefficient on ROOKIECONTRACT * DV2003 indicates that the 1999 CBA reduced highly paid early-career players' salaries by about $650,000. There is little evidence of systematic salary differences based on position as found in Berri *et al.* [10], but this result may be caused by including HEIGHT as an explanatory variable.

The coefficient on 1st indicates that the top paid players were earning large salaries even after controlling for their productivity. The coefficient on 1st is more than twice as large as the coefficient on 2nd and more than triple the coefficient on 3rd in the specification. As for the effects of the 1999 CBA, the coefficient on DV2003 indicates that salaries rose by more than $1 million on average (even after adjusting for inflation). However, the rank-year interaction terms (1st * DV2003, *etc.*), especially in the win share specifications, indicate large gains for complementary players. Comparing 2nd * DV2003 to 2nd indicates that the gains to the second ranked players more than doubled. Similar comparisons indicate that pay for third ranked and, in some specifications, fourth ranked players increased by more than 50%. The gains to star players are much smaller (about one-fourth) and are imprecisely estimated. Hence, the estimation results are consistent with the conjecture that the 1999 CBA shifted the distribution of player pay toward complementary players, particularly the second highest paid players on each team. The results, therefore, may help explain Bill Simmons's observation [1] about the high pay of complementary players, such as Elton Brand and Luol Deng.

5. Conclusions

A formal model for why the rents should accrue to complementary players instead of going to other input suppliers (e.g., coaches) or to team owners is beyond the scope of this short paper, but tournament theory [14] is the implicit basis underlying our conjecture that the individual salary cap redistributed rents to complementary players. In tournament theory, compensation rests not only on productivity but on rank order. In our context, the maximum player salary could be viewed as a mechanism that attenuates the return to being the top ranked player on a team thereby allowing for the redistribution of those rents.

In college sports, economists hypothesize that rents derived from not paying college athletes lead to increased compensation for coaches or to more lavish athletic facilities [15,16]. For example, Andrew Zimbalist (quoted in Nocera 2007 [17]) states, "Since the players don't get paid, you can't just go out and hire the Tom Bradys of college sports, so instead (colleges) throw money at everything else." Although the notion that coaches or others capture the rents generated by unpaid college athletes may be widely accepted, we know of no empirical tests of this hypothesis. The lack of empirical testing is probably the result of there not being any rule changes regarding payment of athletes or other empirical frameworks appropriate for such tests.

In the NBA, however, evidence suggests that coaches have little effect on player performance [18]. Thus it would make little sense to expect rents created from capping individual player salaries to flow to NBA coaches. Under the 1999 CBA, therefore, the most productive NBA resource for which pay could be bid up might have been role players, such as Brand and Deng, who were not earning the league's maximum allowable salary. This paper's findings that imposing maximum player salaries led to a large increase in pay for the second and third highest paid players on NBA teams is consistent with the conjecture that the 1999 CBA led to a shift in rents from star players to complementary players.

Author Contributions: Both authors contributed to the data collection, empirical analysis, and writing of this paper.

Conflicts of Interest: The authors declare no conflict of interest.

References

1. Simmons, B. A Fan-Friendly Solution to Fix the NBA. ESPN.com, 24 February 2010. Available online: http://sports.espn.go.com/espn/page2/story?page=simmons/100224 (accessed on 18 March 2015).
2. Hill, J.R.; Groothuis, P.A. The new NBA collective bargaining agreement, the median voter model, and a Robin Hood rent redistribution. *J. Sports Econ.* **2001**, *2*, 131–144. [CrossRef]
3. Beck, H. For N.B.A. owners, 1999 labor deal was win with regrets. *New York Times*, 3 July 2011; SP6.
4. Kaplan, R.A. The NBA luxury tax model: A misguided regulatory regime. *Columbia Law Rev.* **2004**, *104*, 1615–1650. [CrossRef]
5. Hakes, J.K.; Sauer, R.D. An economic evaluation of the moneyball hypothesis. *J. Econ. Perspect.* **2006**, *20*, 173–186. [CrossRef]
6. Bradbury, J.C. Does the baseball labor market properly value pitchers? *J. Sports Econ.* **2007**, *8*, 616–632. [CrossRef]
7. Jenkins, J.A. A reexamination of salary discrimination in professional basketball. *Soc. Sci. Q.* **1996**, *77*, 594–608.
8. Rod Fort's Sports Data Website. Available online: https://sites.google.com/site/rodswebpages/codes (accessed on 18 March 2015).
9. Basketball-Reference.com. Available online: http://www.basketball-reference.com/ (accessed on 18 March 2015).
10. Berri, D.J.; Brook, S.L.; Schmidt, M.B. Does one simply need to score to score? *Int. J. Sport Finance* **2007**, *2*, 190–205.
11. Berri, D.J.; Brook, S.L.; Frick, B.; Fenn, A.J.; Vicente-Mayoral, R. The short supply of tall people: Competitive imbalance and the National Basketball Association. *J. Econ. Issues* **2005**, *39*, 1029–1041.

12. Ducking, J.; Groothuis, P.A.; Hill, J.R. Minimum pay scale and career length in the NBA. *Ind. Relat. J. Econ. Soc.* **2014**, *53*, 617–635. [CrossRef]
13. Kendall, T.D. Celebrity misbehavior in the NBA. *J. Sports Econ.* **2008**, *9*, 231–249. [CrossRef]
14. Lazear, E.P.; Rosen, S. Rank-order tournaments as optimum labor contracts. *J. Polit. Econ.* **1981**, *89*, 841–864. [CrossRef]
15. Kahn, L.M. Cartel behavior and amateurism in college sports. *J. Econ. Perspect.* **2007**, *21*, 209–226. [CrossRef]
16. Farmer, A.; Pecorino, P. Is the coach paid too much? Coaching salaries and the NCAA cartel. *J. Econ. Manag. Strategy* **2010**, *19*, 841–862. [CrossRef]
17. Nocera, J.; Skybox, U. *New York Times*, 28 October 2007; 38.
18. Berri, D.J.; Leeds, M.A.; Leeds, E.M.; Mondello, M. The role of managers in team performance. *Int. J. Sport Finance* **2009**, *4*, 75–93.

International Journal of
Financial Studies

MDPI

Article

The Long-Term Game: An Analysis of the Life Expectancy of National Football League Players

Ruud Koning [1], Victor Matheson [2,*], Anil Nathan [2] and James Pantano [2]

[1] Department of Economics and Econometrics, Faculty of Economics and Business, University of Groningen, PO Box 800, 9700 AV Groningen, The Netherlands; r.h.koning@rug.nl

[2] Department of Economics and Accounting, College of the Holy Cross, One College Street, Worcester, MA 01610, USA; anathan@holycross.edu (A.N.); JFPANT13@g.holycross.edu (J.P.)

* Author to whom correspondence should be addressed; vmatheso@holycross.edu; Tel.: +1-508-793-2649; Fax: +1-508-793-3710.

Received: 7 February 2014; in revised form: 5 March 2014; Accepted: 10 March 2014; Published: 18 March 2014

Abstract: The National Football League (NFL) has recently received significant negative media attention surrounding the safety of its players, revolving largely around the long term health risks of playing the sport. Recent premature deaths and instances of suicide associated with chronic traumatic encephalopathy and other football related injuries have brought the sport under increased scrutiny. By comparing mortality rates of the general population to mortality rates of players using publically available data from the 1970 and 1994 NFL seasons, we test whether participation in football is significantly harmful to the longevity of the players. We conclude that, in total, players in the NFL have lower mortality rates than the general population. However, there is evidence that line players have higher mortality rates than other players and that those who played more games have higher mortality rates than those who played fewer games.

Keywords: National Football League; premature deaths; survivability; injuries

---

1. Introduction

The National Football League (NFL) has recently been scrutinized about the impact of playing the game on mortality and quality of life. High profile cases such as the suicides of Atlanta Falcons safety Ray Easterling, Chicago Bears defensive back Dave Duerson, and San Diego Chargers linebacker Junior Seau, as well as the tragic premature death of long-time Pittsburgh Steeler Mike Webster, have certainly pushed these issues to the forefront of media attention. Cantu [1] and Samson [2] confirm that both Webster and Seau had chronic traumatic encephalopathy (CTE), and Mecham [3] confirms evidence of CTE in both Duerson and Easterling. CTE is most often caused by severe and repeated head injuries and leads to brain degeneration and dementia [4].

In August 2013, the NFL attempted to settle a lawsuit brought by former players claiming that the league downplayed the risks of concussion-related brain injuries. The NFL agreed to provide $765 million to compensate victims, pay for medical exams for 4500 plaintiffs and other retired players, and engage in medical research [5]. Due to questions regarding the adequacy of the payout, however, the settlement was not granted initial approval by Judge Anita Brody who noted that, " . . . it is difficult to see how the Monetary Award Fund would have the funds available over its lifespan to pay all claimants . . . " [6]. A better understanding of risk factors relating to premature deaths are of interest both to the teams individually, and the NFL collectively.

However, the financial implications go much further than just settling the grievances of past players. The future of the NFL could be at stake through two channels. First of all, the perception already exists that the NFL is a guilty pleasure where spectators enjoy the game at the long-term expense of the health of the participants [7]. Mounting evidence that playing in the NFL causes serious health problems or shortens life could cause a drop in the NFL's popularity similar to what has happened to the sport of boxing [8]. Secondly, due to health concerns there has already been a drop in football participation rates at the youth level. Between 2010 and 2012, a period of heightened awareness of head injuries in the NFL, there was a 6.7% drop in the number of players ages 6 through 14 playing Pop Warner Football, the largest decline in the long history of nation's biggest youth football program [9]. A continued drop in participation would impact the pipeline of players into the NFL as well as future interest in the sport in general.

While anecdotal evidence of players dying prematurely is both alarming and the subject of considerable attention in the popular press, can it be statistically shown that playing in the NFL leads to a lower life expectancy for ex-players? This paper will examine whether NFL players have a higher mortality rate than the general population and will look at which factors affect the mortality of NFL players.

Baron and Rinsky [10] show that former NFL players have a much lower mortality rate than the general population, as well as some other interesting patterns. For example, defensive linemen have higher rates of cardiovascular disease than the general population, and black players were more likely to develop cardiovascular disease than white players. Lehman *et al.* [11] also find that NFL players have lower mortality rates than the general population while having a higher incidence of neurodegenerative mortality. These papers show evidence that high profile deaths can skew the perception of the risk of playing in the NFL.

This paper is related to other papers that examine (excess) mortality in professional sports. Related literature is discussed in Koning and Amelink [12], who show that Dutch professional soccer players have a lower mortality rate than the general Dutch population. Sanchis-Gomez *et al.* [13] and Marijon *et al.* [14] show that mortality among French professional cyclists who participated in the Tour de France is lower than that of the French population. These studies suggest that professional athletes have better health than the average population, increasing longevity.

Our paper adds to the literature by using a flexible probability model developed in Koning and Amelink [12] that can be used to compare NFL mortality rates to those in the general population. In addition, we also use Cox hazard rate models [15], to estimate survival of players at an individual level and to determine the impact of games played, position, and race on player mortality.

Our results show that NFL players have a lower mortality rate than the general population (by race and overall) in both the 1970 and 1994 seasons. In the 1970 season, offensive and defensive line players have higher mortality rates than those in the other positions, and non-white players have higher mortality rates than white players. Most importantly, players who played more than 2 seasons worth of games have higher mortality rates than those that have played less. In the 1994 season, line players have higher mortality rates than those who are in the skilled positions, but other factors are not statistically significant.

Sections 2 and 3 describe the data and models used in the study, while Section 4 displays the results. Section 5 concludes and discusses some more potential research.

2. Data

We examine player cohorts for two seasons, 1970 and 1994, and include all players who appeared in at least one game during either of those seasons. The 1970 cohort consists of 1244 players, and the 1970 cohort has 1600 players. The 1970 season was chosen for two reasons. First, using an older season ensures that survival probabilities in the general population become sufficiently low and observational data with the players have enough natural attrition to be meaningful. Second, 1970 was the first season after the National Football League-American Football League merger effectively doubling sample size of players and also ensuring that players in the sample had relatively standardized equipment and playing conditions. It should be noted, however, that the data set includes all players who played during the 1970 season, not just who started their careers in the 1970 season, so the player statistics

Int. J. Financial Stud. **2014**, *2*, 168–178

may include games played prior to the merger. The 1994 season included to see whether changes in the game, including better equipment as well and stronger and faster players, has had an effect on player mortality. In addition, the 1994 cohort has, anecdotally, experienced an abnormally large number of premature deaths.

Most of the player data for the 1970 and 1994 NFL seasons was collected on "Pro-Football-Reference.com" [16] which has season-by-season statistics for every player to have appeared in an NFL game as well as dates of birth and death for all players. Data on race was revealed through online picture searches of the players. Players were placed into one of three positional categories: skill positions, which include wide receivers, tight ends, quarterbacks, and running backs; line positions, which include players on the offensive and defensive lines, who tend to be much larger and heavier than other players; and other, which includes mostly defensive players who are not linemen plus some punters and kickers.

Table 1 lists summary statistics for the 1970 and 1994 seasons. There were 1244 total players who participated in the 1970 season and 1600 players in the 1994 season with identifiable race data. Approximately two-thirds of the players who played in the 1970 season are white, but by 1994 only one third of the players are white. Across both whites and non-whites, the percentage of players still alive is very similar. This survival rate equality is not reflective of the survival rates of whites and non-whites in the general population where non-whites have experienced significantly higher mortality rates than whites. For both seasons, the average age was in the mid-twenties at the relevant time. The split between positions was generally even in 1970, with a shift towards line players and away from skill players in 1994. Players in 1994 participated in more games over their career than those in 1970, at least in part due to the regular season being extended by two games. In 1970, whites played about a season's more worth of games over a career than non-whites, but in 1994 non-whites played more than two-and-a-half more seasons than whites. This fact is also reflected in the percentage of whites and non-whites that played at least two season's worth of games in 1970 compared to 1994.

Table 1. Summary Statistics.

Season	Variable	All	White	Non-White
	Alive in 2012	1091	690	401
1970	Alive in 2012 (%)	87.7	88.35	86.61
	Dead in 2012	153	91	62
	Dead in 2012 (%)	12.3	11.65%	13.39%
	Age in 1970	25.1	25.45	24.52
	White (%)	64.98	-	-
	Line (%)	33.2	36.24	28.08
	Skill (%)	33.92	32.01	37.15
	Other (%)	32.88	31.75	34.77
	Games Played	95.73	100.12	88.35
	Long Career (%) (27+ career games played)	88.1	91.66	82.07
	Alive in 2012	1559	523	1036
	Alive in 2012 (%)	97.44	97.03	97.64
	Dead in 2012	41	16	25
	Dead in 2012 (%)	2.56	2.97	2.36
1994	Age in 1994	25.79	27.13	25.11
	White (%)	33.69	-	-
	Line (%)	38.12	35.99	39.21
	Skill (%)	26.12	27.83	25.26
	Other (%)	35.75	36.18	35.53
	Games Played	108.18	80.68	122.16
	Long Career (%) (27+ career games played)	88.62	74.03	96.04

3. Models

The following survival model is an adaptation of the one developed in Koning and Amelink [12] for Dutch soccer players. The idea is to compare the expected survival of individuals based on the general population at the appropriate time to the observed survival of NFL players. Let x be the age of an individual, t be the base (or starting) year, and let s be the number of years after t. Also, let N (x, t) be the number of individuals of age x alive at time t. Therefore, N (t), which is the number of individuals (regardless of age) that are alive at time t is as follows.

$$N(t) = \sum_x N(x, t)$$

$$(1)$$

Let $(x, t, t + s)$ be the probability that an individual of age x at time t survives to time $t + s$ (or in other words, survives s years from time t). So, for example, an individual survives one year from time t with a probability P $(x, t, t + 1)$. As such, the probability that an individual of age x at time t survives to time $t + s$ can be represented by the product of successive one-year probabilities.

$$P(x, t, t + s) = \prod_{n=1}^{s} P(x, t + n - 1, t + n)$$

$$(2)$$

The expected number of individuals of age x alive at time t that are still alive at $t + s$ can be represented as follows.

$$N(x + s, t + s) = N(x, t) * P(x, t, t + s)$$ $$(3)$$

Using equation (1) above, the total number of individuals alive at time t that are expected to be alive at time $t + s$ is the following.

$$N(t + s) = \sum_x N(x + s, t + s)$$

$$(4)$$

N $(t + s)$, the expected number of individuals that survive to time $t + s$ can then be compared to the actual number of players that survive to time $t + s$ to see if these players experience different longevity than the general population of a similar age composition.

This approach compares mortality between the population of NFL players, and the US population in general. Besides that, we also examine whether observable risk factors influence the individual risk of mortality within the population of NFL players. To do so, we estimate a Cox proportional hazard model was also constructed to determine factors that impact mortality with the following equation.

$$\lambda(t) = \lambda_0(t)e^{(\beta'x)}$$ $$(5)$$

The covariates used are games played, position played, and race. In this case, the baseline hazard $(\lambda_0(t))$ captures mortality among NFL players in general. In this specification, we do not allow for time-varying covariates. That is, we only allow for individual specific covariates. The relevant time scale is the age of the player, and we allow for censored observation using the usual start/stop approach as in Therneau and Grambsch [15] and Fox [17].

4. Results

The expected number of survivors, classified by age, based on population probabilities of survival and the model above can be calculated in order to make a comparison with the actual numbers of players (also classified by age) surviving. Tables 2 and 3 list the comparisons overall and by race for 1970 and 1994.

Table 2. Actual Survival and Expected Survival (1970 Season).

Age	All				White				Non-White			
	Number	Alive	Expected Alive	P-value	Number	Alive	Expected Alive	P-value	Number	Alive	Expected Alive	P-value
21	116	107	94.97	0	64	60	53.41	0.03	38	34	25.46	0
22	186	176	150.28	0	110	107	90.65	0	71	64	46.42	0
23	168	156	133.71	0	94	87	76.36	0	67	62	42.67	0
24	150	126	117.35	0.09	90	81	71.92	0.02	53	39	32.82	0.09
25	154	137	118.18	0	97	85	76.09	0.03	52	48	31.23	0
26	100	89	75.11	0	64	58	49.18	0.01	35	30	20.35	0
27	104	87	76.29	0.02	64	54	48.07	0.11	37	30	20.79	0
28	75	63	53.61	0.01	56	46	41.02	0.17	19	17	10.29	0
29	60	50	41.68	0.02	43	35	30.63	0.18	16	14	8.34	0
30	47	34	31.62	0.54	28	22	19.33	0.31	19	12	9.48	0.26
31	32	29	20.76	0	24	22	16	0.01	7	6	3.33	0.06
32	18	12	11.21	0.81	15	10	9.61	1	3	2	1.35	0.59
33	14	10	8.33	0.43	13	9	7.96	0.78	1	1	0.43	0.43
34	10	9	5.66	0.05	9	8	5.24	0.09	1	1	0.4	0.4
35	4	4	2.14	0.13	4	4	2.2	0.13	-	-	-	-
36	4	4	2.01	0.37	4	1	2.07	0.36	-	-	-	-
38	1	1	0.44	0.44	1	1	0.45	0.45	-	-	-	-
42	1	0	0.3	1	1	0	0.31	1	-	-	-	-

Table 3. Actual Survival and Expected Survival (1994 Season).

Age	All				White				Non-White			
	Number	Alive	Expected Alive	P-value	Number	Alive	Expected Alive	P-value	Number	Alive	Expected Alive	P-value
19	1	1	0.97	1	1	1	0.97	1	-	-	-	-
20	7	7	6.79	1	-	-	-	-	7	7	6.62	-
21	66	66	63.97	0.27	14	14	13.61	1	52	52	49.09	0.12
22	163	163	157.78	0.01	37	37	35.93	0.63	126	126	118.68	0
23	255	249	246.46	0.49	62	61	60.12	1	193	188	181.28	0.05
24	202	195	194.85	1	43	42	41.62	1	159	153	148.88	0.25
25	175	170	168.41	0.69	49	48	47.32	1	126	122	117.54	0.15
26	154	149	147.79	0.84	48	44	46.23	0.1	106	105	98.45	0.01
27	135	130	129.16	1	44	43	42.26	1	91	87	84.1	0.32
28	116	113	110.62	0.38	50	47	47.88	0.47	66	66	60.66	0.01
29	87	87	82.68	0.02	48	48	45.82	0.17	39	39	35.62	0.05
30	58	57	54.92	0.37	32	31	30.44	1	26	26	23.59	0.17
31	70	68	66.02	0.44	45	44	42.66	0.73	25	24	22.5	0.51
32	44	41	41.31	0.75	20	19	18.88	1	24	22	21.41	1
33	30	28	28.03	1	18	17	16.92	1	12	11	10.6	1
34	14	12	13.01	0.26	9	8	8.42	0.45	5	4	4.37	0.49
35	7	7	6.47	1	6	6	5.59	1	1	1	0.86	1
36	4	4	3.67	1	4	4	3.7	1	-	-	-	-
37	9	9	8.22	1	7	7	6.44	1	2	2	1.68	1
38	1	1	0.91	1	1	1	0.92	1	-	-	-	-
39	2	2	1.8	1	1	1	0.91	1	1	1	0.82	-

For the 1970 cohort for almost all ages, the actual number of NFL players still alive in 2013 is statistically significantly higher (at the 5% level) than what is predicted by the population survival model. In 1994, the actual numbers of players surviving by age is also generally higher than expected, but the observed number of survivors is typically not statistically significantly larger than the expected number of survivors. There are two possible explanations for this result. First, most of the players from the 1994 cohort are still alive and therefore the statistical power of this test to uncover differences in survival rates is lower than statistical tests for the 1970 cohort. Second, it is possible that the increasing size, speed and strength of players in the modern game subjects more recent players to higher long-term risks. Thus, the much higher survival rates of older NFL veterans may not be replicated in more recent age groups. That being said, it is still notable that the number of deaths in this cohort is below the number of deaths that would be expected in the general population, which goes against the popular notion that this cohort had a particularly high mortality rate.

Figure 1a–f charts overall survival by year *versus* the number expected to survive by year. For both the cohorts, the actual survival plot is above the expected survival plot. In fact, the only time when the actual survival plot is even within the 95% confidence interval of survival is for white players who played in the 1994 season. Perhaps this reflects the unusual mortality of that particular season, but the confidence interval is very wide due to the fact that one would not expect there to be many deaths for such a young cohort.

Table 4 reports the results of the Cox hazard rate model. In both seasons, the baseline hazard is that of non-white line players with a career length in the bottom 10% of their respective cohort. For both 1970 and 1994 this means career lengths of approximately two NFL seasons or less. A negative coefficient implies a lower hazard rate of death (compared to the baseline hazard) and a positive coefficient implies increased risk. The results are quite striking in for the 1970 cohort. White players have a 33% lower hazard rate (which is the odds ratio reported in Table 4 subtracted from one) than a non-white players. Skill position players and other players have a 38% and 46% lower hazard rate, respectively, than the baseline. Both of these results are in line with the findings of Baron and Rinsky [10] who found that defensive linemen and black players both experienced high rates of cardiovascular disease. It is acknowledged, however, that individuals with body types similar to line players are more susceptible to ailments such as cardiovascular disease solely due to their body mass alone. Of most interest, however, is that the players with more than 2 seasons of experience have a striking 347% higher hazard rate than those players who played in the NFL in 1970 but had only a short NFL career. Other specifications of games played are also robust to this analysis.

Table 4. Cox Hazard Rate Model Results.

Attribute	1970 Season			1994 Season		
	Coeff.	Odds Ratio	*P*-Value	Coeff.	Odds Ratio	*P*-Value
White	−0.4	0.67	0.02	0.03	1.03	0.93
Skill	−0.48	0.62	0	−1.65	0.19	0.01
Other	−0.63	0.54	0.01	−0.34	0.71	0.3
Long career	1.5	4.47	0.01	−0.3	0.74	0.6

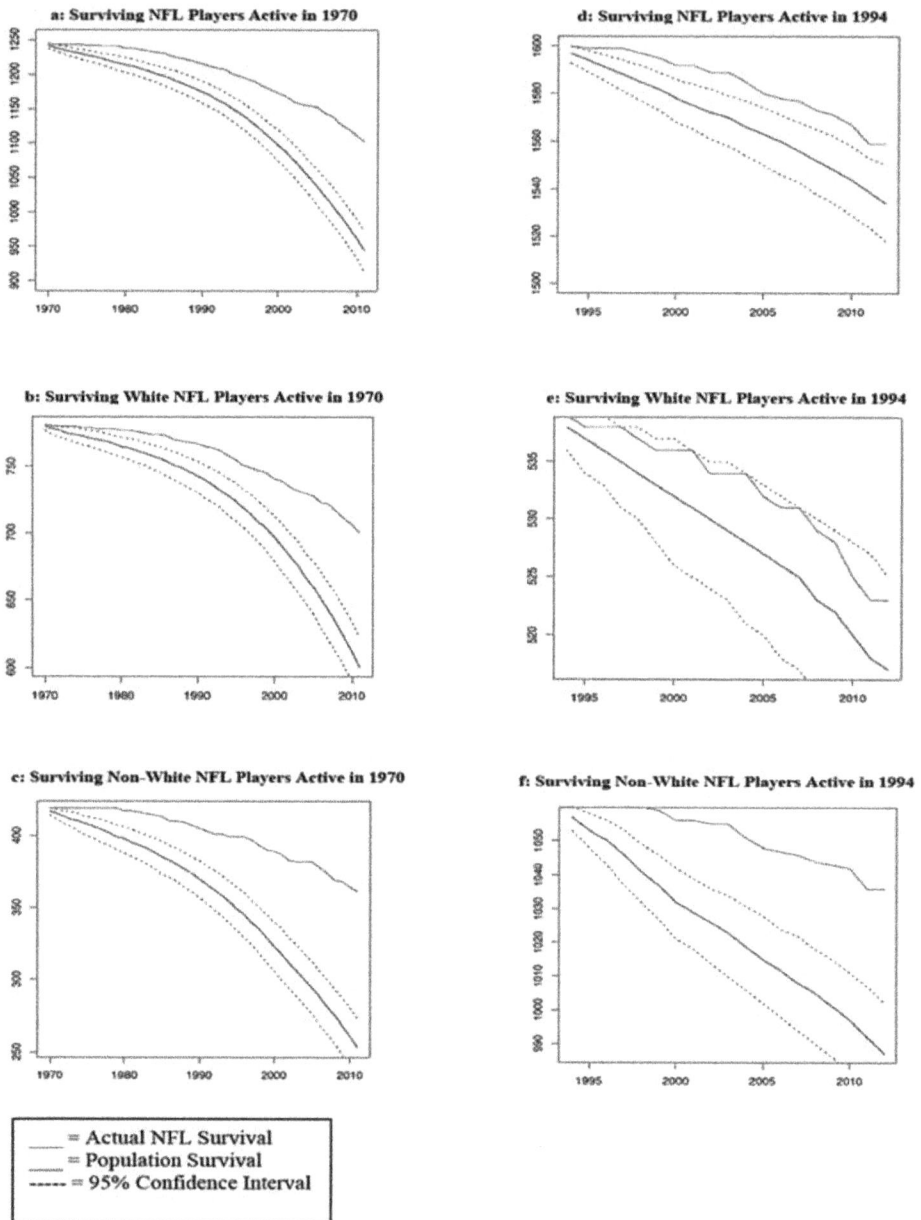

Figure 1. Surviving NFL Players by Year and Date.

The 1994 cohort produces substantially different results. White players no longer exhibit lower mortality than non-white players. In addition, only skill position players have a significantly different hazard rate than linemen. Here, skill position players have an 81% lower hazard than the baseline, but other players are not statistically significantly different. Players with short NFL careers no longer

Int. J. Financial Stud. **2014**, *2*, 168–178

exhibit lower mortality than players with longer careers. However, as discussed previously, not enough time has elapsed since that season to estimate effects with a high degree of precision.

5. Conclusions

It has been popular recently, based on anecdotal evidence and a few very high profile cases, to conclude that players in the NFL may have higher mortality rates than the general population. Using data on the actual survivability of NFL players and comparing it to the expected population survival of individuals in a similar time period, it seems that NFL players have higher survivability (lower mortality) rates than the general population. However, there is evidence that mortality rates are higher for line players, who may take more abuse or have different physical characteristics than other players. There is also evidence that those players who play more than two seasons worth of games also face higher mortality rates than other players. So, compared to the overall population, NFL players survive longer, but when compared with their peers who do not play many games, those that play more do not survive as long.

There are some limitations to this study. For example, a claim may be made that the difference in expected *versus* actual survivability may be overestimated due to the fact that players in the NFL may be healthier (they are elite athletes, after all) or have better access to quality health care in general [18,19]. Income differences could also lead to differential health effects, and Weir *et al.* [20] show that NFL player earnings are substantially higher than that of the general population. If it can be assumed, however, that players with longer careers have similar general background characteristics (such as innate health, body mass index, life circumstances, *etc.*) as those without career longevity, then this study provides clear evidence that the rigors of the NFL may actually shorten life expectancy, but not to an extent that NFL players have a higher mortality rate than the general population.

We have also not touched on any specific ailments or any injury history (such as concussions), which could cause quality of life issues that differ from the general population. This issue is often conflated with mortality, but may be even more important and need elucidating. In terms of purely examining life expectancy, however, our results suggest that this is another example of confirmation bias in the NFL, where a presupposition is backed by strong anecdotal evidence but no statistical backing [21].

The NFL, however, has cause to be alarmed by the variation in the mortality rates between players at different positions. This study provides some evidence that certain types of players (*i.e.*, linemen) die faster than others, potentially cutting into the future pipeline of these types of players. Even more concerning is the evidence that players with the shortest careers have the longest life expectancy. A general public distaste of knowing that a source of entertainment may actually shorten the lives of those who participate in it the most, may hurt interest in the NFL in the long term, which will subsequently negatively impact the NFL's bottom line.

Acknowledgments: We thank James Hamilton for his excellent research assistance. We also thank the College of the Holy Cross for funding the Holy Cross Economics and Accounting summer research assistant program.

Author Contributions: All listed authors contributed equally in all aspects of the paper including writing, editing, literature review, data collection and analysis.

Conflicts of Interest: The authors declare no conflict of interest.

References

1. Cantu, R.C. Chronic Traumatic Encephalopathy in the National Football League. *Neurosurgery* **2007**, *61*, 223–225. [CrossRef]
2. Samson, K. Former NFL Player Junior Seau Had CTE. *Neurol. Today* **2013**, *13*, 12–15.
3. Mecham, M. Paul Oliver: Latest in a string of NFL suicides. Available online: http://fox13now.com/2013/09/26/paul-oliver-latest-in-a-string-of-nfl-suicides/ (accessed on 26 September 2013).

Int. J. Financial Stud. **2014**, *2*, 168–178

4. McKee, A.C.; Stein, T.D.; Nowinski, C.J.; Stern, R.A.; Daneshvar, D.H.; Alvarez, V.E.; Lee, H.-S.; Hall, G.; Wojtowicz, S.M.; Baugh, C.M. The Spectrum of Disease in Chronic Traumatic Encephalopathy. *Brain* **2012**, *136*, 43–64.

5. Smith, S. NFL and ex-players reach deal in concussion lawsuit. Available online: http://www.cnn.com/2013/08/29/health/nfl-concussion-settlement/ (accessed on 30 August 2013).

6. Farrar, D. Judge Anita Brody denies preliminary approval for NFL concussion settlement. Available online: http://nfl.si.com/2014/01/14/nfl-concussion-lawsuit-settlement-2/ (accessed on 14 January 2014).

7. Reilly, R. Football Getting Harder to Watch. Available online: http://espn.go.com/nfl/story/_/id/9932209/nfl-becoming-guilty-pleasure (accessed on 6 November 2013).

8. Donnelly, P. On boxing: Notes on the past, present and future of a sport in transition. *Curr. Psychol.* **1988**, *7*, 331–346. [CrossRef]

9. Fainaru, S.; Fainaru-Wada, M. Youth Football Participation Drops. Available online: http://espn.go.com/espn/otl/story/_/page/popwarner/pop-warner-youth-football-participation-drops-nfl-concussion-crisis-seen-causal-factor (accessed on 13 November 2013).

10. Baron, S.; Rinsky, R. *NIOSH Mortality Study of NFL Football Players: 1959–1988*; HETA 88-085; Centers for Disease Control, National Institute for Occupational Safety and Health: Cincinnati, OH, USA, 1994.

11. Lehman, E.J.; Hein, M.J.; Baron, S.L.; Gersic, C.M. Neurodegenerative Causes of Death Among Retired National Football League Players. *Neurology* **2012**, *79*, 1970–1974. [CrossRef]

12. Koning, R.H.; Amelink, R. Medium-Term Mortality of Dutch Professional Soccer Players. *Econ. Lab. Relat. Rev.* **2012**, *23*, 55–68. [CrossRef]

13. Sanchis-Gomar, F.; Olaso-Gonzalez, G.; Corella, D.; Gomez-Cabrera, M.C.; Vina, J. Increased Average Longevity among the "Tour de France" Cyclists. *Int. J. Sports Med.* **2011**, *32*, 644–647. [CrossRef]

14. Marijon, E.; Tafflet, M.; Antenero-Jacquemin, J.; El Helou, N.; Berthelot, G.; Celermajer, D.S.; Bouhouin, W.; Combes, N.; Hermine, O.; Empana, J.-P.; *et al.* Mortality of French participants in the Tour de France (1947–2012). *Eur. Heart J.* **2013**, *34*, 3145–3150. [CrossRef]

15. Therneau, T.M.; Grambsch, P.M. *Modeling Survival Data: Extending the Cox Model*; Springer: New York, NY, USA, 2000.

16. Pro Football Reference. Available online: http://www.pro-football-reference.com/ (accessed on 1 June 2012).

17. Fox, J. Cox Proportional-Hazards Regression for Survival Data—Appendix to *An R and S-PLUS Companion to Applied Regression*. Available online: http://cran.r-project.org/doc/contrib/Fox-Companion/appendix-cox-regression.pdf (accessed on 31 January 2014).

18. Andersen, L.B.; Schnohr, P.; Schroll, M.; Hein, H.O. All-Cause Mortality Associated With Physical Activity During Leisure Time, Work, Sports, and Cycling To Work. *Arch. Int. Med.* **2000**, *160*, 1621–1628. [CrossRef]

19. Lee, I.-M.; Paffenbarger, R.S. Associations of Light, Moderate, and Vigorous Intensity Physical Activity with Longevity: The Harvard Alumni Health Study. *Am. J. Epidemiol.* **2000**, *151*, 293–299. [CrossRef]

20. Weir, D.R.; Jackson, J.S.; Sonnega, A. *National Football League Player Care Foundation Study of Retired NFL Players*; University of Michigan Institute for Social Research: Ann Arbor, MI, USA, 2009.

21. Bursik, P.B. Behavioral Economics in the NFL. In *The Economics of the National Football League*; Springer: New York, NY, USA, 2012; pp. 259–276.

International Journal of
Financial Studies

MDPI

Article

The Effects of the Clock and Kickoff Rule Changes on Actual and Market-Based Expected Scoring in NCAA Football

Kenneth Linna [1], Evan Moore [1,*], Rodney Paul [2] and Andrew Weinbach [3]

[1] Department of Economics, Finance, and Marketing, Auburn University at Montgomery, P.O. Box 244023, Montgomery, AL 36124, USA; klinna@aum.edu

[2] Department of Finance, Syracuse University, 810 Nottingham Road, Syracuse, NY 13224, USA; rpaul01@syr.edu

[3] Department of Finance and Economics, Coastal Carolina University, P.O. Box 261954, Conway, SC 29528-6054, USA; aweinbac@coastal.edu

* Author to whom correspondence should be addressed; emoore1@aum.edu; Tel.: +1-334-244-3364; Fax: +1-334-244-3792.

Received: 28 February 2014; in revised form: 1 April 2014; Accepted: 9 April 2014; Published: 16 April 2014

Abstract: Clock rule changes were introduced in the 2006 season with the goal of reducing the average duration of the game; these changes were reversed in 2007. In addition, in 2007 the kickoff rule was changed to create more excitement and potentially more scoring. We examine what happened to actual and expected scoring during these National Collegiate Athletic Association (NCAA) football seasons. The clock rule change in 2006 led to lower scoring which was not fully encompassed in the betting market, leading to significant returns to betting the under. Multiple rule changes in 2007 led to volatility in the betting market that subsided by season's end.

Keywords: rule change; amateur sports; scoring; gambling; betting; market efficiency; prediction markets

JEL Classification: L83

1. Introduction and Literature Review

Regulation and rule changes are instituted in business and in sports for a variety of reasons. In some cases regulation is introduced to protect consumers or players. In other cases, changes in rules occur to simply increase revenues, lower costs, or achieve both simultaneously. When rules or regulations are changed, it provides a natural framework to perform a case study as to the financial ramifications of the changes to determine if they match the stated goals of the policy. Just as important and interesting is to study the market expectations of rule and regulation changes through financial markets. Understanding how financial markets performed before, during, and after rule changes provides insights into the thoughts and minds of investors and allows for testing of the efficient markets hypothesis.

The testing of stock price movements as they relate to accounting rules and regulation date back to the classic study of Fama *et al.* [1], where the role of new information on security prices was formally investigated. Over time, many research papers have investigated the role of regulation announcements and the implementation of regulations on stock prices (*i.e.*, Binder [2,3] and Schwert [4]). These studies on stock price movements relate back to the testing and further understanding of the implications of the efficient markets hypothesis (Fama [5,6]). Specific examples of where case studies of financial regulation on stock prices were performed include investigation of Sarbanes-Oxley (Jain and Rezaee [7];

Zhang [8]), Garn-St. Germain (Millon-Cornett and Tehranian [9]), Glass-Steagall Act: Section 20 (Cyree [10]) and reviews of bank regulation in general (Millon-Cornett [11] and Carow and Kane [12]).

Financial research into investor sentiment and feelings has been performed on a variety of fronts and is summarized in a literature review by Lucey and Dowling [13]. The role of investor feelings has been used to study stock market response to sporting events, where stock prices are examined and abnormal returns (if any) are calculated following sports contests. These findings have led to considerable debate in the literature surrounding market returns related to English football (soccer) on the London Stock Exchange (FTSE) (Ashton *et al.* [14,15] and Klein *et al.* [16]). Bell *et al.* [17] used a similar concept to study stock market returns of publicly-traded soccer clubs as it related to match results and expectations. Edmans *et al.* [18] studied sports sentiment and stock returns for major international sporting events such as the world cup and international cricket, rugby, and basketball.

It is also possible to study the expected and actual influences of rule changes on gameplay within a sport itself through the investigation of sports betting markets. Sport betting markets are simple financial markets which allow market participants to wager on the outcome of a game or the total number of points scored in a game through prices expressed as point spreads, totals, or odds.

Although sports gambling markets are simple in nature, they are quite popular, with estimates for annual sports wagering by the American Gaming Association being over $3 Billion in Nevada (legally) and $380 Billion illegally across the United States [19]. Rule changes that impact the style of play can be investigated through changes in betting market prices before games are actually played and changes to these prices can be tracked over time. In general, financial studies of sports wagering markets have been unable to reject market efficiency for large overall samples of games across sports. Sports betting markets were assumed to behave under the balanced book hypothesis, where point spreads and totals were assumed to be set to even the betting dollars on each side of the wagering proposition. If achieved, this would allow the sports book to profit without risk in this market, due to the commission charged on bets (a bet $11 to win $10 rule). Recently, Levitt [20] challenged the balanced book hypothesis showing that sports books are not balanced as bettors consistently prefer the favorite in data from a betting market tournament. Paul and Weinbach [21] confirmed this result with betting market percentage data on sides (wagers on a team compared to the point spread) and totals (over/under bets) through data from actual on-line sports books.

Two studies that investigated betting market expectations related to rule changes in sports were Paul *et al.* [22] and Paul and Paul [23]. When the National Football League introduced the two-point conversion rule, it was found that the frequency of posted point spreads increased around key numbers such as three (a field goal differential). The increase in frequency of these key numbers outpaced the frequency of game outcomes of three by a wide (statistically significant) margin [22]. This change in policy by the sports book likely helped them from the greater likelihood of being "middled" (losing both sides of a wager) in NFL games.

Another instance where the betting market adjusted to a rule change was in the National Hockey League. When the NHL eliminated ties in games by adding a shootout, the totals (over/under) market went through a major adjustment. Overall scoring increased by nearly a goal-per-game, but the betting market actually over-adjusted early in the season. This led to profitable returns for under bettors [23] in the totals market. By the end of the season, however, the market appeared to completely adjust to the new rule changes as expected scoring mimics actual scoring within the league.

Two significant rule changes were undertaken by the National Collegiate Athletic Association (NCAA) Football Rules Committee for the 2006 and 2007 seasons. In 2006, the clock rule was introduced to change the timing on plays and reduce the length of college football games. In 2007, this rule was reversed, but the committee also introduced a new kickoff rule to induce more returns by moving the kickoff spot back by 5 yards (from the 35 to the 30 yard line). The goal of our research is twofold. We examine the impact of these rule changes to determine how they impacted actual and expected scoring. We study if the rule changes had the anticipated impact on scoring by investigating total points scored (actual scoring) and the betting market total on the game (expected scoring). We aim to

Int. J. Financial Stud. **2014**, *2*, 179–192

determine if the market anticipated the changes in scoring and how quickly it adjusted. When the 2006 rule was reversed and the new rule was introduced in 2007, we examine which effect had a bigger impact on scoring, the clock rule or the kickoff rule. The overall goal of this research is to determine how the NCAA football rule changes impacted on-field play and how the betting market reacted to these changes before, during, and after their initiation.

The NCAA is the governing body for major collegiate sports in the United States, with supervision of different sports for over 1200 colleges and universities. Major collegiate football is referred to as Division I, and this division currently has two subdivisions: the Football Bowl Subdivision (FBS) and the Football Championship Subdivision (FCS). The FCS uses a single-elimination playoff system to determine a champion; the teams participating in the playoffs are selected by an NCAA FCS committee. The FBS is significantly different from the FCS in two ways: (1) the FBS has a series of bowl games at the end of the regular season; and (2) the champion is not determined by the NCAA but rather by the Bowl Championship Series (BCS). While the authority of the BCS is sanctioned by the NCAA, this is the only NCAA sporting division that does not finish with an NCAA championship [24].

To expand upon the details of the rule changes and to obtain some semblance of the expectations related to these rule changes, consider the following details and quotes related to the rule changes in college football for the 2006 and 2007 seasons. Prior to the start of the 2006 college football season, the NCAA Football Rules Committee made "recommendations concerning the length of the game" in an attempt to shorten the duration of football games [25]. The recommendations included:

(1). Starting the clock on kickoffs when the foot touches the ball, not the returning team;
(2). Starting the clock when the ball is ready for play on a change of possession; and
(3). Shorten the halftime allowance from 20 to 15 minutes.

According to NCAA Football Rules Committee chair and football coach at Pittsburg State Charles Broyles, "We looked at quite a few proposals to shorten the game … Starting the clock on the change of possession is probably our biggest change. We think this is a good change and that this will help reach our goals in this area [26]." Broyles was correct; Steve Wieberg wrote, "College football's rules makers got what they wanted: a faster, shorter game." He reports, of the opening week games, that in 2006 31 of the 72 games were completed in 3 hours or less, with four lasting as long as 3.5 hours. In 2005 only five of 52 games completed in 3 hours or less; 13 went 3.5 hours or longer [26].

Coaches noticed that these changes had an impact on play. West Virginia coach Rich Rodriguez stated, "Normally, in most games, you have 12 or 13 possessions. We had 10 on offense." He went on to say, "So you've really got to make things happen offensively." In a similar vein, South Florida coach Jim Leavitt noted, "People are very aware of the speed of the game right now [26]."

However, early in the season there did not appear to be many coaches viewing the changes as particularly problematic to game management. Texas Tech coach Mike Leach noted, "I don't think they're too hard to work around." However, he also added, "I just think it's dumb to shorten these games that have been a perfectly good length for years and years [26]."

Coach Leach's assessment was ultimately shared by other coaches. According to Steve Wieberg [27], "Coaches hated the moves (the clock rule changes)." The NCAA rules oversight panel voted to eliminate the clock rule changes " … used last year that helped shave 14 minutes off of game times [28]." Additionally, the panel decided to change the kickoff from the 35 yard line to the 30 yard line beginning with the 2007 season. According to the football rules committee spokesman, Ty Halpin, the proposed justifications for changing the kickoff rule in NCAA football include creating " … more opportunities for what the committee feels is one of the most exciting plays in a game, and we're not really sure, but it may increase scoring, too [29]." This was mirrored by Dave Parry, national coordinator of NCAA football officiating, who stated, "It will create a little more excitement, and we'll get a little more movement of the ball [30]."

A number of coaches have commented regarding this rule change on scoring. According to Kentucky head coach Rich Brooks, "It's going to be one of the most significant rule changes to come around in a decade . . . . You're going to see scoring averages go up because of this rule change." Auburn head coach Tommy Tubberville stated, "It will add more points to the scoreboard [31]." Mark Nelson, Louisville's special teams coach, made the following prediction: "Add about seven points to the total score of every game [32]."

Regardless of the sport, rule changes are usually made with specific intentions. Often, rules are changes with the goal of increasing interest in the game. Bannerjee and Swinnen [33] investigated FIFA's introduction of the golden goal rule, to "stimulate more attractive football" and Bannerjee *et al.* [34] noted that the NHL's rule change regarding overtime results was done "in an effort to stimulate a more exciting and entertaining style of play."

The effects of rule changes in sports have covered a variety of other topics as well. These include the effects of rule changes on competitive balance in Formula 1 racing [35], Japanese professional baseball [36], and across North American major sports leagues [37]. Still other works address the effects of rule changes on strategy and play style; Guedes and Machado [38] examine the effect of FIFA's increase in the number of points awarded to winning a game on offensive efforts and Moschini [39] finds that the change led to a statistically significant increase in the expected number of goals. Banjeree *et al.* [34] investigate the NHL's overtime rules change on play style during the both the regular and overtime periods. McCannon [40] investigates the effect of the three-point line being extended on men's NCAA basketball finding that the change led to a decrease in three-point shooting and scoring along with a decrease in the percentage of successful two-point shots. Regarding rule changes and penalties, Witt [41] evaluates the effects of FIFA's rule change regarding the increase in offenses qualifying as red-card worthy on the number of the number and types of penalties called.

This paper presents results concerning the effects of NCAA Football rule changes in 2006 and 2007 on total scoring, scoring margin, and competitiveness of the games. These results are then compared to what happened in the financial (betting) market for college football totals. The outcomes between actual and expected scoring due to the rule changes are compared. These results are then compared to the preseason predictions of the rules committee, the officials, and a variety of coaches. The next section provides analyses of the actual scoring data and findings. Section 3 presents the results from the totals betting market. Section 4 discusses the findings and concludes the paper.

2. Actual Scoring and Outcomes

The actual scoring data used in this study consists of the final scores from NCAA Division I football games in the 2005, 2006 and 2007 seasons. This includes all 2308 games involving at least one Division I Football Bowl Subdivision (FBS) team. The complete data set will be used in the overview provided in the next section. However, 364 matchups, totaling 1092 games, were played in each of the three seasons. To avoid dependence issues, most of the analysis was conducted using difference scores for these repeat matchups.

Table 1 presents summary statistics for the scores of the three seasons in six categories. In five of the six categories the total scoring decreased from 2005 to 2006 then increased with the 2007 season to a higher mean than that of the 2005 season. The exception was BCS bowl games as scoring in 2007 did not exceed that of the 2005 season.

Table 1. Summary scoring statistics for the 2005–2007 seasons.

Category	Statistic	2005 Mean (StDev)	2006 Mean (StDev)	2007 Mean (StDev)
All games	Total score	52.60 (17.20)	47.53 (16.12)	55.41 (18.69)
	Winning score	35.11 (12.14)	32.51 (11.46)	36.46 (12.32)
	Losing score	17.49 (9.852)	15.02 (9.448)	18.95 (10.99)
	Margin	17.62 (13.90)	17.49 (13.47)	17.51 (14.00)
	N	718	792	798
Non-conference games (reg. season)	Total score	52.13 (16.92)	47.88 (15.37)	54.20 (18.05)
	Winning score	36.97 (13.33)	34.76 (12.19)	38.05 (13.28)
	Losing score	15.16 (9.484)	13.13 (9.381)	16.15 (10.56)
	Margin	21.80 (15.77)	21.63 (15.39)	21.91 (15.81)
	N	239	303	316
Conference games (reg. season)	Total score	52.61 (17.18)	47.03 (16.57)	56.09 (18.97)
	Winning score	34.22 (11.48)	31.06 (10.89)	35.40 (11.43)
	Losing score	18.39 (9.661)	15.97 (9.186)	20.69 (10.89)
	Margin	15.83 (12.46)	15.08 (11.47)	14.71 (11.78)
	N	451	457	450

Category	Statistic	2005 Mean (StDev)	2006 Mean (StDev)	2007 Mean (StDev)
Bowl games	Total score	56.61 (19.80)	51.44 (16.54)	57.69 (20.63)
	Winning score	33.75 (10.32)	32.09 (8.917)	35.56 (13.06)
	Losing score	22.86 (11.73)	19.34 (10.54)	22.12 (11.00)
	Margin	10.89 (9.814)	12.75 (10.37)	13.44 (12.55)
	N	28	32	32
BCS Bowl games	Total score	63.75 (14.5)	56.40 (17.60)	60.00 (12.27)
	Winning score	34.75 (6.500)	36.20 (8.044)	40.00 (10.08)
	Losing score	29.00 (8.832)	20.20 (12.34)	20.00 (6.892)
	Margin	5.750 (5.550)	16.00 (11.14)	20.00 (12.15)
	N	4	5	5
Non-BCS Bowl games	Total score	55.42 (20.55)	50.52 (16.51)	57.26 (21.98)
	Winning score	33.58 (10.92)	31.33 (9.000)	34.74 (13.54)
	Losing score	21.83 (11.99)	19.19 (10.43)	22.52 (11.66)
	Margin	11.75 (10.19)	12.15 (10.34)	12.22 (12.46)
	N	24	27	27

The margin of victory was relatively stable for non-conference games over the period while the margin decreased in conference games. It was also relatively stable for non-BCS bowl games in both the 2006 and 2007 seasons. However, note that the margin of the BCS bowl games increased from 5.5 points in 2005 to 16 points in 2006, and then to 20 points in 2007. This coincides with the winning teams increasing scoring and the losers decreasing scoring in these games, on average.

These increasing scoring margins coincided with a decline in average BCS bowl game television ratings, from Nielson ratings of 13.98 in 2005–2006 to 9.52 in 2007–2008. This corresponds with the findings of Salaga and Tainsky [42] in their work on Neilson ratings for BCS games; their results indicate that increases in the margin at a given quarter decrease ratings. The previously mentioned study investigates the uncertainty of outcome hypothesis while Grimshaw *et al.* [43] examines TV audiences for the NCAA men's basketball Final Four games based on a consumer theory model. Future research into the factors affecting TV audiences for these games is warranted due to the financial stakes; the 2011–2014 television deal generates $155 million per season for the BCS while the upcoming contract is estimated at $470 million per year [42]. Given six BCS games in the upcoming season then the per-game figure is approximately $78.3 million. For the sake of comparison, the NCAA men's basketball tournament's television deal currently averages $771 million per year [43]. However, excluding any play-in games there are 63 games in this tournament resulting in a per-game figure of approximately $12.2 million. Table 2 presents summary statistics for each of the BCS automatic bid conferences. This summary information reveals that the margin of victory decreased for these conferences between the 2005 and 2007 seasons. In five of the six conferences this is driven by increases in the losers' scores.

Table 2. Scoring statistics for Bowl Championship Series (BCS) Automatic Bid Conferences.

		2005 Mean (StDev)	2006 Mean (StDev)	2007 Mean (StDev)			2005 Mean (StDev)	2006 Mean (StDev)	2007 Mean (StDev)
ACC	Total score	46.64 (15.05)	40.98 (16.82)	47.71 (13.93)	Big Ten	Total score	56.14 (13.78)	46.50 (17.59)	52.64 (17.97)
	Winning score	30.56 (11.21)	27.13 (10.36)	30.22 (9.150)		Winning score	37.05 (9.838)	31.68 (11.67)	33.30 (10.43)
	Losing score	16.09 (7.940)	13.84 (10.02)	17.49 (7.959)		Losing score	19.09 (9.215)	14.82 (9.848)	19.34 (10.27)
	Margin	14.47 (12.29)	13.29 (11.51)	12.73 (10.01)		Margin	17.95 (13.18)	16.86 (12.53)	13.95 (10.28)
	N	45	45	45		N	44	44	44
Big 12	Total score	54.35 (16.74)	52.02 (17.26)	62.18 (19.28)	PAC-10	Total score	59.25 (16.82)	44.84 (13.52)	53.47 (17.16)
	Winning score	37.10 (13.47)	33.02 (10.61)	41.00 (12.51)		Winning score	37.85 (12.20)	30.80 (9.236)	33.98 (10.96)
	Losing score	17.24 (9.013)	19.00 (9.314)	21.18 (11.13)		Losing score	21.40 (9.139)	14.04 (8.116)	19.49 (9.134)
	Margin	19.86 (15.65)	14.02 (10.03)	19.82 (13.75)		Margin	16.45 (13.48)	16.76 (10.93)	14.49 (10.62)
	N	49	49	49		N	40	45	45
Big East	Total score	49.54 (16.05)	49.21 (17.57)	53.36 (18.46)	SEC	Total score	43.88 (17.60)	42.20 (13.58)	53.90 (20.25)
	Winning score	34.39 (10.21)	31.68 (9.813)	33.89 (12.64)		Winning score	28.92 (11.18)	26.71 (9.115)	33.27 (11.93)
	Losing score	15.14 (9.679)	17.54 (9.879)	19.46 (9.693)		Losing score	14.96 (9.460)	15.49 (7.901)	20.63 (10.81)
	Margin	19.25 (11.76)	14.14 (8.902)	14.43 (12.92)		Margin	13.96 (10.93)	11.22 (10.32)	12.63 (10.40)
	N	28	28	28		N	49	49	49

Int. J. Financial Stud. **2014**, *2*, 179–192

Table 3 presents the results of two-tailed t-tests for the mean differences in each category from zero. The results from the repeated matchups are used in this analysis. The total, winning, and losing scores are all significantly lower at less than the 1 percent level in the 2006 season compared to the values for 2005. The total score decreased by 4.66 points per game. However, the margin of victory did not change significantly. This suggests that the implementation of the clock rule changes led to decreased scoring but did not have any statistically significant effect on the margin of victory. A comparison of the 2007 and 2005 seasons reveals that the kickoff rule changes led to total scoring increasing by 2.93 points per game, with this being driven primarily by increases in the losers' score by 1.77 points. This supports the results discussed in regard to Table 2. These results are statistically significant at the 5 percent level.

Table 3. Tests of significance for changes in scoring across the 2005–2007 seasons.

	t-statistic	*p-value*	*Mean Difference*
2006–05 total score	−3.858	0.000	−4.659
2006–05 winning score	−3.274	0.001	−2.571
2006–05 losing score	−3.036	0.003	−2.088
2006–05 margin	−0.569	0.570	−0.484
2007–05 total score	2.253	0.025	2.934
2007–05 winning score	1.421	0.156	1.168
2007–05 losing score	2.391	0.017	1.766
2007–05 margin	−0.693	0.489	−0.599

Degrees of freedom for all tests equals 363.

3. Financial Market Expectations and Outcomes

The next step in our analysis is to examine the financial (betting) market reaction to the rule changes in NCAA football. As was seen in the previous section, scoring declined in 2006 when the NCAA introduced rules aimed at shortening the length of the game. When these rules were reversed in 2007, the NCAA also introduced a change in the placement of the kickoff which was likely to result in better starting field position for the offense. The combination of these rule changes in 2007 led to increased scoring beyond the levels seen in 2006 and even in 2005 (prior to the rule changes).

Given that the betting market for college football is a simple financial market, it is possible to trace the rule changes in college football to their implications on prices. In the case of analyzing rules that impact scoring, the totals markets is the market we will investigate. The totals market is commonly known as the over/under market and is a simple financial market where bettors can wager on whether the combined score of both teams will be greater than or less than the posted number by the sports book. Previous studies of market efficiency in the college football wagering market has shown the market to be efficient in the aggregate, although simple strategies of wagering on the under at the highest totals has been shown to reject market efficiency [44].

The question pertaining to this study is if the betting market adjusted to these rule changes and, if it did, how quickly did the market adjust? Given that the rule changes were announced in advance, sports book managers and bettors alike were able to analyze and hypothesize about the impact of these changes before the season began. Even if the rule changes could not be incorporated immediately, it is likely if one assumes market efficiency (and the incentives present in the market) that the impact of the rule changes would quickly be realized and prices would adjust to their unbiased values.

To begin, we will examine the year prior to the rule changes, 2005, and then compare these results to 2006 and 2007. We examine what happened each season in the aggregate to allow for enough observations to perform possible meaningful tests on market efficiency. It is important to understand that small sample sizes in sports betting markets can reveal unreliable results as noted in Osborne [45]. Given that we are interested in specific years and are attempting to understand the speed of adjustment of the market in those seasons, we believe the relatively large number of games in a college football season (over four times as many games as an NFL season), we believe the data set is large enough to provide insight on the issues of interest. The following table shows the mean and standard deviation of the total for each season. For each year studied, the first four weeks of the season and the results for the season as a whole are presented.

Table 4. Descriptive statistics summarizing totals by season.

Week	2005 Season Mean Total (Standard Deviation)	2006 Season Mean Total (Standard Deviation)	2007 Season Mean Total (Standard Deviation)
Week 1	50.55(5.71)	47.52(4.96)	49.36(5.16)
Week 2	51.53(6.31)	47.71(5.91)	50.32(7.48)
Week 3	51.32(5.63)	47.68(5.08)	53.08(8.77)
Week 4	51.60(7.43)	47.05(6.37)	53.88(8.23)
Entire Season	51.96(7.08)	47.73(6.52)	54.50(8.27)

The results of Table 4 above illustrate that when the new clock rules were introduced in 2006, totals immediately fell. In Week 1, the mean total fell by 3 points. By Week 4, the mean total was around 4.5 points lower than it was at the same time in 2005. By the end of the season, the mean total was over 4 points lower than in 2005. The standard deviation of the total also fell by around a half point. Compared to the actual scoring results, where scoring on the average in 2006 was shown to decrease nearly 5 points compared to 2005, the average total fell, but not quite as much as actual scoring.

In 2007, with the change back of the clock rules and the movement of the kickoff from the 35 to 30 yard line, there appeared to be a bit more confusion in the totals market. Totals only rose slightly (compared to 2006) in Weeks 1 and 2, but jumped by Week 3 to levels beyond those seen in 2005. Overall, totals rose by about 7 points compared to 2006 and about 2.5 points compared to 2005. The standard deviation also rose in 2007. This compares quite closely to the actual change in scoring, which would be predicted under the efficient markets hypothesis, as actual scoring rose by nearly 8 points from 2006 to 2007 and was between 2.5 and three points greater than it was in 2005.

The next step in analyzing the market is to compare betting market results during these years to see how simple strategies of wagering on the over or the under-performed before and after the college football rule changes. The following three tables show the over and under record in the 2005, 2006, and 2007 seasons. For each season, individual week results for Weeks 1–4 and the overall season results are shown. Table 5 includes information on the number of overs, unders, and pushes, the under win percentage, and the log likelihood ratio test for a fair bet (win percentage equal 50%) from Even and Noble [46].

Before the rule changes, in 2005, overs and unders split nearly evenly in the totals betting market. With the introduction of the new clock rules in 2006, the under did considerably better than the over. The 53.16% win percentage of simply betting the under was great enough to reject the null hypothesis of a fair bet at the 10% level. This result is not overly surprising given the previous findings in this paper, as the actual amount of scoring fell by a greater amount than the betting market total, resulting in more wins on betting the under.

Table 5. Over/Under Records and Fair Bets by Season.

Week	Overs	Unders	Pushes	Under %	Log Likelihood Fair Bet
Week 1	20	25	1	56.56%	0.5567
Week 2	25	23	0	47.92%	0.0834
Week 3	23	21	0	47.73%	0.0909
Week 4	21	23	0	52.28%	0.0909
2005 Season	336	330	6	49.55%	0.0541

a. 2005 NCAA Football Season—Over/Under Record.

Week	Overs	Unders	Pushes	Under %	Log Likelihood Fair Bet
Week 1	23	21	0	47.73%	0.0909
Week 2	24	26	0	52.00%	0.0800
Week 3	21	29	0	58.00%	1.2855
Week 4	20	28	1	58.33%	1.3396
2006 Season	334	379	9	53.16%	2.8420*

b. 2006 NCAA Football Season—Over/Under Record.

Week	Overs	Unders	Pushes	Under %	Log Likelihood Fair Bet
Week 1	19	27	1	58.70%	1.3984
Week 2	32	18	1	36.00%	3.9729**
Week 3	21	27	2	56.25%	0.7520
Week 4	33	14	1	29.79%	7.9051***
2007 Season	339	370	12	52.19%	1.3559

c. 2007 NCAA Football Season—Over/Under Record.

Note: The log likelihood test statistics have a chi-square distribution with one degree of freedom. Critical values are 2.706 ($\alpha = 0.10$), 3.841 ($\alpha = 0.05$), 6.635 ($\alpha = 0.01$).

In 2007, multiple rule changes appeared to cause some confusion in the betting market. There was great volatility early in the season, with some weeks where the over dominated and other weeks where the under outperformed the over. In Weeks 2 and 4, scoring was so high that the over won enough to reject the null hypothesis of a fair bet at the 5% level in Week 2 and at the 1% level in Week 4. By the end of the season, however, unders did slightly better than overs, but not nearly as well as in 2006. It appeared that uncertainty reigned early in the 2007 college football season due to the multiple rule changes, but by the end of the season the total pretty well reflected the actual amount of scoring that happened in college football games.

Detailed betting data available from Sportsinsights [47] can shed further light in terms of what happened in the totals market during these seasons. Sportsinsights publishes the betting percentages on each side of the wagering proposition for college football and other sports. This information was used to test the balanced book hypothesis (the notion that sports books set prices to even the betting action on each side of the proposition). The balanced book was soundly rejected in college football [21] in addition to other sports. Although this study and more recent research illustrated that the book was not balanced, the point spreads and totals studied were still shown to serve as an unbiased forecast of game outcomes (despite clear betting biases toward the favorites and overs).

Table 6. Betting Public Perception: Betting Percentage on the Over.

Year	Average % on Over	Standard Deviation on Over
2005	63.12	16.25
2006	65.69	15.09
2007	64.08	13.75

Table 6 presents the mean percentage bet on the over for the 2005–2007 seasons. As is clearly seen in the table, bets on the over are much more popular than bets on the under. Wagers on the over received greater than 60% of the betting action throughout the sample period. In 2006, the percentage bet on the over rose to 65.69%, an increase of nearly 2.5% over 2005. Due to the clock rule changes, totals fell in 2006. These lower totals likely proved to be even more tempting to over bettors, due to their pre-existing bias that already existed for wagering on the over. This increase in betting percentage on the over also likely contributed to the under being a winning wager overall during the 2006 NCAA football season. In 2007, with the rise in the total due to the reversal of clock rules and the introduction of the kickoff rule, the percentage bet on the over fell by about 1.5% compared to where it was in 2007, which was slightly higher than it was in 2005, but the betting market went back to a more even split between overs and unders during that season.

Overall, the effects of the clock rules were anticipated by the book makers as they lowered totals, but bettors did not fully grasp the effects. This led to slightly higher totals than there should have been and a winning season for under bettors in 2006. The reversal of the clock rules and the introduction of the new kickoff rule in 2007 was met with some confusion in the early season by both bookmakers and bettors. By the end of the season, it appeared that the market adjusted to the new rules in place for college football.

4. Discussion and Conclusions

The results reveal that the clock rule changes instituted in the 2006 season and the kickoff rule change that began with the 2007 season had an effect on scoring in Division I Football Bowl Subdivision (FBS) games. Using 2005 as the base year, we found that the clock rule changes of 2006 decreased total scoring by 4.66 points per game, with the winners' scores decreased by 2.57 points and the losers' scores decreased by 2.09 points on average. These results are statistically significant at the 5 percent level or lower. The elimination of the clock rule changes for the 2007 season allowed us to compare the effects of the kick rule change against the scoring of the 2005 season. We found that total scoring increased by 2.93 points per game, with the losers' scores earning the bulk of the increase, receiving 1.77 points on average. Nevertheless, neither rule change had a statistically significant effect, at any generally accepted level, on the margins of victory during these seasons. It is not clear from the results that the games are more competitive on average. This suggests that other rule changes may be necessary to reduce the margin.

In the over/under market for college football, the total fell due to the clock rule changes in 2006. These lower totals spurred more betting action on the over during this season (due to the behavioral bias which already exists in this market where bettors prefer wagering on the over rather than the under) and led to under bets significantly outperforming over bets. The financial market for NCAA football totals betting showed much volatility early in the season in 2007, due to the reversal of the clock rules and the introduction of the kickoff rule. By the end of the season, however, market expectations and actual results meshed with general findings of market efficiency with the slight (but normal compared to previous studies) behavioral bias of bettors toward the over.

The predictions of the kick rule change by various coaches were generally correct; scoring averages increased with this rule. However, statements by coaches that it may have a "huge impact" or be one the "most significant" rule changes appear a bit strong, at least in regard to scoring. Our results suggest that the timing rule changes had a much stronger impact on scoring in these games.

Overall, rule changes in sports change the manner of play on the field, influence the way fans respond to the sport, and influence financial (betting) markets related to the game. The major rule changes which occurred in college football in 2006 and 2007 led to changes in scoring that were mostly predictable ex-ante by sports book managers, but still led to some biased results due to the behavioral preferences of market participants.

Acknowledgments: The authors thank the participants at the sports economics session of the 45th annual Academy of Economics and Finance conference for their helpful comments.

Author Contributions: All listed authors contributed equally to the research completed and writing of the paper.

Conflicts of Interest: The authors declare no conflicts of interest.

References

1. Fama, E.; Fisher, L.; Jensen, M.; Roll, R. The Adjustment of Stock Prices to New Information. *Int. Econ. Rev.* **1969**, *10*, 1–21. [CrossRef]
2. Binder, J. Measuring the Effects of Regulation with Stock Price Data. *Rand J. Econ.* **1985**, *16*, 167–183. [CrossRef]
3. Binder, J. The Event Study Methodology Since 1969. *Rev. Quant. Finance Account.* **1998**, *11*, 111–137. [CrossRef]
4. Schwert, G. Using Financial Data to Measure Effects of Regulation. *J. Law Econ.* **1981**, *24*, 121–158.
5. Fama, E. Efficient Capital Markets: A Review of the Theory and Empirical Work. *J. Finance* **1970**, *25*, 383–417. [CrossRef]
6. Fama, E. Efficient Capital Markets II. *J. Finance* **1991**, *46*, 1575–1617. [CrossRef]
7. Jain, P.; Rezaee, Z. The Sarbanes-Oxley Act of 2002 and Capital Market Behavior: Early Evidence. *Contemp. Account. Res.* **2006**, *23*, 629–654. [CrossRef]
8. Zhang, I. Economic Consequences of the Sarbanes-Oxley Act of 2002. *J. Account. Econ.* **2007**, *44*, 74–115. [CrossRef]
9. Millon-Cornett, M.; Tehranian, H. An Examination of the Impact of the Garn-St. Germain Depository Institutions Act of 1982 on Commercial Banks and Savings and Loans. *J. Finance* **1990**, *45*, 95–111. [CrossRef]
10. Cyree, K. The Erosion of the Glass-Steagall Act: Winners and Losers in the Banking Industry. *J. Econ. Bus.* **2000**, *52*, 343–363. [CrossRef]
11. Millon-Cornett, M. Stock Market Reactions to the Depository Institutions Deregulation and Monetary Control Act of 1980. *J. Bank. Finance* **1989**, *13*, 81–100. [CrossRef]
12. Carow, K.; Kane, E. Event-Study Evidence of the Value of Relaxing Longstanding Regulatory Restraints on Banks: 1970–2000. *Q. Rev. Econ. Finance* **2002**, *42*, 439–463. [CrossRef]
13. Lucey, B.; Dowling, M. The Role of Feelings in Investor Decision-Making. *J. Econ. Surv.* **2005**, *19*, 211–237. [CrossRef]
14. Ashton, J.; Gerrard, B.; Hudson, R. Economic Impact of National Sporting Success: Evidence from the London Stock Exchange. *Appl. Econ. Lett.* **2007**, *10*, 283–785.
15. Ashton, J.; Gerrard, B.; Hudson, R. Do National Soccer Results Really Impact on the Stock Market? *Appl. Econ.* **2011**, *43*, 3709–3717. [CrossRef]
16. Klein, C.; Zwergel, B.; Heiden, S. On the Existence of Sports Sentiment: The Relation between Football Match Results and Stock Index Returns in Europe. *Rev. Manage. Sci.* **2009**, *3*, 191–208. [CrossRef]
17. Bell, A.; Brooks, C.; Matthews, D.; Sutcliffe, C. Over the Moon or Sick as a Parrot? The Effects of Football Results on a Club's Share Price. *Appl. Econ.* **2012**, *44*, 3435–3452. [CrossRef]
18. Edmans, A.; Garcia, D.; Nurli, O. Sports Sentiment and Stock Returns. *J. Finance* **2007**, *62*, 1967–1998. [CrossRef]
19. American Gaming Association. Available online: http://www.americangaming.org/industry-resources/research/fact-sheets/sports-wagering (accessed on 19 March 2014).
20. Levitt, S. Why are gambling markets organized so differently from financial markets? *Econ. J.* **2004**, *114*, 223–246. [CrossRef]
21. Paul, R.J.; Weinbach, A.P. Sportsbook Behavior in the NCAA Football Betting Market: Tests of the Traditional and Levitt Models of Sportsbook Behavior. *J. Prediction Markets* **2009**, *3*, 21–37.

22. Paul, R.J.; Weinbach, A.P.; Mahar, J. The Betting Market Response to the 2-Point Conversion in the NFL. *J. Bus. Econ. Persp.* **2007**, *33*, 98–110.

23. Paul, R.J.; Paul, K.K. Market Reaction to a Structural Change: The Totals Market of the NHL. *Bus. Res. Yearb.* **2007**, *14*, 53–59.

24. Wallace, R. FBS vs. FCS. Available online: http://www.differencebetween.net/miscellaneous/difference-between-fbs-and-fcs/ (accessed on 19 March 2014).

25. NCAA Press Release. Available online: http://football.refs.org/rules/NCAA2006pr.html (accessed on 19 March 2014).

26. Wieberg, S. Teams get adjusted to rules shortening game. *USA Today*, 4 September 2006.

27. Wieberg, S. NCAA rules committee proposes reworking football time-saving rules. *USA Today*, 14 February 2007.

28. NCAA Press Release. Available online: http://fs.ncaa.org/Docs/PressArchive/2007/Playing%2BRules/NCAA%2BFootball%2BRules%2BCommittee%2BVotes%2BTo%2BRestore%2BPlays%2BWhile%2BAttempting%2BTo%2BMaintain%2BShorter%2BOverall%2BGame%2BTime.html (accessed on 19 March 2014).

29. Associated Press. Available online: http://sports.espn.go.com/ncf/news/story?id=2835266 (accessed on 19 March 2014).

30. Brunt, C. College Football Changes Kickoff Rule. Available online: http://www.washingtonpost.com/wp-dyn/content/article/2007/08/16/AR2007081601365.html (accessed on 19 March 2014).

31. Hood, S. New Kickoff Rule Gets (Special) Teams Attention. Available online: http://sports.yahoo.com/ncaaf/news?slug=rivals-146383&prov=rivlas&typs=lgns (accessed on 19 March 2014).

32. Dodd, D. Kick Back and Enjoy as Returns Grow More Intriguing. Available online: http://www.sportsline.com/collegefootball/story/10323027 (accessed on 19 March 2014).

33. Banerjee, A.N.; Swinnen, J.F.M. Does a Sudden Death Liven Up the Game? Rules, Incentives, and Strategy in Football. *Econ. Theor.* **2004**, *23*, 411–421. [CrossRef]

34. Banerjee, A.N.; Swinnen, J.F.M.; Weersink, A. Skating on Thin Ice: Rule Changes and Team Strategies in the NHL. *Can. J. Econ.* **2007**, *40*, 493–514. [CrossRef]

35. Mastromarco, C.; Runkel, M. Rule Changes and Competitive Balance in Formula One Motor Racing. *Appl. Econ.* **2009**, *41*, 303–314.

36. La Croix, S.J.; Kawaura, A. Rule Changes and Competitive Balance in Japanese Professional Baseball. *Econ. Inq.* **1999**, *37*, 353–356.

37. Fort, R.; Lee, Y.H. Structural Change, Competitive Balance, and the Rest of the Major Leagues. *Econ. Inq.* **2007**, *45*, 519–532. [CrossRef]

38. Guedes, J.C.; Machado, F.S. Changing Rewards in Contests: Has the Three-Point Rule Brought More Offense to Soccer? *Empir. Econ.* **2002**, *27*, 607–630. [CrossRef]

39. Moschini, G. Incentives and Outcomes in a Strategic Setting: The Three-Points-for-a-Win System in Soccer. *Econ. Inq.* **2010**, *48*, 65–79. [CrossRef]

40. McCannon, B.C. Strategic Offsetting Behavior: Evidence from National Collegiate Athletic Association Men's Basketball. *Contemp. Econ. Policy* **2011**, *29*, 550–563. [CrossRef]

41. Witt, R. Do Players React to Sanction Changes? Evidence from the English Premier League. *Scot. J. Polit. Econ.* **2005**, *52*, 623–640. [CrossRef]

42. Salaga, S.; Tainsky, S. The effects of outcome uncertainty, scoring, and pregame expectations on Neilson ratings for Bowl Championship Series games. *J. Sport. Econ.* **2013**. [CrossRef]

43. Grimshaw, S.; Sabin, R.P.; Willes, K.M. Analysis of the NCAA men's Final Four TV audience. *J. Quant. Anal. Sport.* **2013**, *9*, 115–126.

44. Paul, R.J.; Weinbach, A. Bettor Preference and Market Efficiency in Football Totals Markets. *J. Econ. Financ.* **2005**, *29*, 409–415. [CrossRef]

45. Osborne, E. Efficient markets? Don't bet on it. *J. Sport. Econ.* **2001**, *2*, 50–61. [CrossRef]

Int. J. Financial Stud. **2014**, *2*, 179–192

46. Even, W.E.; Noble, N.R. Testing efficiency in gambling markets. *Appl. Econ.* **1992**, *24*, 85–88. [CrossRef]
47. Sportsinsights. Available online: http://www.sportsinsights.com (accessed on 19 March 2014).

International Journal of
Financial Studies

MDPI

Article

Systematic Positive Expected Returns in the UK Fixed Odds Betting Market: An Analysis of the Fink Tank Predictions

Babatunde Buraimo [1], David Peel [2] and Rob Simmons [2,*

[1] Management School, University of Liverpool, Liverpool L69 7ZX, UK; b.buraimo@liverpool.ac.uk
[2] Management School, Lancaster University, Lancaster LA1 4YX, UK; d.peel@lancaster.ac.uk
* Author to whom correspondence should be addressed; r.simmons@lancaster.ac.uk;
  Tel.: +44(0)-015-245-942-34.

Received: 12 October 2013; in revised form: 15 November 2013; Accepted: 28 November 2013;
Published: 4 December 2013

Abstract: We report striking evidence of semi-strong inefficiency in the UK fixed-odds football betting market using a reputable newspaper tipster which offers probabilities of match outcomes rather than simple result indicators. Betting on the Fink Tank probabilities of home wins across 10 bookmakers, when there are positive expected returns, would have generated positive returns in each of the seasons from 2006–07 to 2011–12 for a variety of different betting strategies. These returns could have been enhanced by employing the best odds from a greater number of bookmakers. However, the fact that pure arbitrage bets have existed for years and appear to last for several hours or days suggest they are in practice not exploitable to a magnitude that poses any threat to bookmakers.

Keywords: inefficiency; football betting; fixed odds; Fink Tank

JEL Classification: L83

---

1. Introduction

It is now well recognized in the literature that betting markets are important for testing market efficiency as pointed out by Thaler and Ziemba [1], they possess the property that each asset or bet has a well-defined termination point at which its value becomes certain. As a consequence, the problems that arise in determining the expected value of future fundamentals are mitigated. Betting markets share many of the other characteristics of asset markets, in particular large numbers of investors (bettors), with readily available cheap sources of information.

There have been numerous studies of the efficiency of the fixed odds football betting market in the UK and elsewhere since the first study of the efficiency of the fixed odds betting in the UK market by Pope and Peel [2]. These authors examined odds from four bookmakers in the 1981–82 season and reported evidence of weak form inefficiency, that is the profitability of a trading rule based purely on bookmakers' posted odds. They also reported the apparent existence of a few pure arbitrage opportunities in the absence of the 10% betting tax at that time. That entails placing bets on the home, away and draw outcome with different bookmakers and winning with certainty, assuming payout is honoured.

Subsequent analyses have documented the existence of mispricing as well as the apparent existence of pure arbitrage possibilities in European fixed-odds football betting markets [3–9]. There are numerous papers that have investigated market efficiency in other sports betting markets such as horse racing, National Football League, greyhounds, National Hockey League, Major League Baseball and National Basketball Association (see Sauer [10] and Williams [11] for surveys). The broad conclusion of the empirical studies is that market efficiency appears violated in various periods but there were no systematic violations and that overall the markets analyzed appear efficient when attitude to risk is appropriately accounted for.

Overall, the reported results from the literature on European football betting suggest that mispricing of odds has occurred over many seasons, particularly in the latter period. However Levitt [12] shows that by systematically setting the "wrong" prices in a manner that takes advantage of bettor preferences, bookmakers can increase profits (see also Humphreys [13], and Paul and Weinbach [14]). However, Levitt also notes that there are constraints on the magnitude of this distortion, since bettors who know the "correct" price can generate positive returns if the posted price deviates too much from the true odds. Consequently, evidence of mispricing that does not lead to betting strategies that can generate positive expected returns is irrelevant from the bookmakers' perspective.

Overall, the view of Forrest and Simmons [15] on statistical models of fixed-odds betting markets seems a good summary of previous work. Forrest wrote "Notwithstanding the apparent potential for employing a statistical model to secure positive returns late in the season, the literature reviewed so far has tended to find difficulty in establishing potential for using statistical modelling to secure positive as opposed to merely less negative returns" ([15], p. 436).

Our purpose in this paper is to provide more striking and firm evidence of semi-strong inefficiency in the UK fixed odds betting market than has been previously reported. We find evidence of systematic positive returns in the English Premier League football based on the predictions of the Fink Tank, (also presented as Castrol Predictor) published weekly in the *The Times* (on Saturday and online at [16]). Constantinou and Fenton [17] analyse data for the Fink Tank for the 2011/12 season as a predictor of outcomes of matches relative to other predictors. However, they do not examine the potential for generating abnormal returns.

The Fink Tank predictions are based on a statistical model that uses time-weighted shots and goals data to generate an attack and defence ranking for each club. The number of goals scored by a club in a match depends on the attack rating of the club and the defence rating of the opposition. There is also a home advantage rating, which allows for the fact that clubs score more goals when playing at home. An early version of the Fink Tank model appeared as Graham and Stott [18].

The Fink Tank predictions are reported in the form of the probabilities of the home, draw and away outcome. This is unusual as tipsters normally just report 'most likely' match outcomes. Forrest and Simmons [5] reported remarkably poor predictive performance of three newspaper tipsters. Later, Forrest *et al.* [19] demonstrated the superior predictive ability of UK bookmakers over an elaborate statistical model in forecasting English League match results across all four tiers of English football.

We examine Fink Tank probabilities in conjunction with the odds of 10 bookmakers over the 2006–07 to 2011–12 Premier League seasons. We find systematic positive returns in each year obtained from a variety of different betting strategies based on betting on the home win. Given that the predictions of Fink Tank are readily available and positive returns have persisted for so many years, so that bettors or bookmakers have had time to learn of the value of the predictions, our findings appear to be of interest.

We also examine in more detail bets that appear to offer pure, paper, arbitrage profits. Numerous such bets exist each week and can be readily found by employing free internet comparisons of fixed-odds bookmaker sites. Of course, if these opportunities were exploitable they would constitute evidence of inefficiency under any definition and raise issues about both bookmaker and bettor rationality. However, it is well known that bookmakers need only balance their books to make a risk-free profit. With a balanced book, bookmakers do not necessarily care about odds from other bookmakers and arbitrage does not necessarily imply irrationality [9]. We should stress, though, that the balanced book assumption has been challenged recently [13].

Int. J. Financial Stud. **2013**, *1*, 168–182

2. Expected Returns from the Fink Tank Model

Our data set comprises the Fink Tank predicted probabilities of all possible outcomes of 1669 matches in the English Premier League, the top division of English football, over the 2006–07 to 2001–12 seasons together with the odds set by 10 bookmakers (Bet365, BWin, Gamebookers, Interwetten, Ladbrokes, Sportingbet, William Hill, StanJames, BETVICTOR, Blue Square). In Table 1 we report some summary statistics for the difference in maximum and minimum odds as a proportion of minimum odds.

Table 1. Differences in maximum and minimum odds as a ratio of minimum odds.

Statistics	Home odds	Away odds	Draw odds
N	1669	1669	1669
Mean	0.232	0.289	0.158
St. deviation	0.115	0.161	0.099

We note that there is a mean difference of 23.2%, 28.9% and 15.8% between the best and worst odds posted for home, away and draw odds respectively. Clearly, placing bets with more than one bookmaker can increase expected returns or decrease losses substantially, ceteris paribus. To illustrate we randomly assumed we bet solely with either William Hills or Ladbrokes. In Table 2 we report the number of times they had the best odds.

Table 2. William Hill's and Ladbrokes's odds *versus* best odds by other bookmakers.

WH or LB versus other bookmakers	N
WH or LB's home odds > other BM's	75
WH or LB's away odds > other BM's	51
WH or LB's draw odds > other BM's	87

LB—Ladbrokes, WH—William Hill, and BM—best bookmaker's odds.

The expected return, for a one unit stake based on the Fink Tank probabilities is given by

$$\mu = pO - (1 - p) \tag{1}$$

where p is the Fink Tank probability and O is the highest odds of the 10 bookmakers. In Table 3 we report the summary statistics for the expected returns for a one unit stake based on the Fink Tank probabilities for home, away and draw employing the best bookmaker odds for our data sample. We follow the literature on European football betting in offering average returns from simulations rather than statistical tests as applied in the literature on North American sports betting.

Table 3. Expected returns—for home win, away win and draw.

	N	Mean	Median	St. dev.	Minimum	Maximum
			Home			
Expected return ≤ 0	837	−0.118	−0.096	0.098	−0.674	0.000
Expected return > 0	832	0.164	0.110	0.183	0.000	1.880
Expected return	1669	0.023	0.000	0.203	−0.670	1.880
			Away			
Expected return ≤ 0	746	−0.149	−0.120	0.125	−0.890	0.000
Expected return > 0	923	0.251	0.170	0.263	0.000	2.825
Expected return	1669	0.072	0.035	0.292	−0.890	2.825
			Draw			
Expected return ≤ 0	1519	−0.157	−0.150	0.089	−0.813	0.000
Expected return > 0	150	0.125	0.050	0.277	0.000	2.650
Expected return	1669	−0.131	−0.142	0.143	−0.813	2.650

Over the sample period the Fink Tank probabilities and best bookmaker odds implied that we would bet on 832 home matches with an average expected return of 16.4%, 923 away matches with an expected return of 25.1% and 150 draws with an expected return of 12.5%. The largest expected home return of 18.8% occurred in the match Swansea *versus* Manchester United when the Fink Tank probability of a home win was $p = 0.36$ and best odds 7/1. In fact Manchester United won the match with a 1-0 away win.

For matches where the expected return is greater than zero we consider a number of betting strategies. The first betting strategy is to stake one unit on each outcome where expected return is positive. We report the results for each season and actual returns to this betting strategy in Table 4.

We observe that betting on one unit on each home team when expected return was positive would have generated a positive return in all seasons except 2008/9 with an average return of 10.75%. The actual returns to a one unit stake on away matches were negative (mean of −8.1%) but positive for draws with volatile returns across seasons. We conjecture that the Fink Tank probabilities deal with home advantage differently to bookmakers. Since home teams win in almost 50% of games, they are more likely to be favourites than away teams. Some studies have found evidence for favourite-longshot bias in European fixed odds betting markets [3]. To the extent that bookmakers are prone to this bias and the Fink Tank predictions avoid such bias then it is possible to derive positive returns from betting on home teams using the Fink Tank. However, the Fink Tank predictions deliver substantial losses from betting on away teams and this may be due to misclassification of results between draws and away wins.

Table 4. Returns to a unit stake on home, away and draw when expected returns are positive and bet on home team benchmark.

Season	Stake	Winning bets	Losing bets	Wins	Profit	Return (%)
			Home			
2006–07	132	65	67	85.04	18.04	13.67
2007–08	143	63	80	86.75	6.75	4.72
2008–09	122	53	69	68.59	−0.41	−0.34
2009–10	151	68	83	101.24	18.24	12.08
2010–11	150	74	76	100.49	24.49	16.33
2011–12	134	61	73	95.33	22.33	16.66
Total	832	384	448	537.44	89.44	10.75
			Away			
2006–07	130	31	99	75.08	−23.92	−18.40
2007–08	189	47	142	91.66	−50.34	−26.63
2008–09	133	44	89	122.05	33.05	24.85
2009–10	145	27	118	64.54	−53.46	−36.87
2010–11	161	34	127	132.18	5.18	3.22
2011–12	165	39	126	140.75	14.75	8.94
Total	923	222	701	626.26	−74.74	−8.10
			Draw			
2006–07	41	12	29	30.85	1.85	4.51
2007-08	19	8	11	30.90	19.9	104.74
2008–09	12	3	9	9.00	0.00	0.00
2009–10	25	3	22	9.8	−12.2	−48.80
2010–11	20	6	14	19.90	5.90	29.50
2011–12	33	10	23	36.65	13.65	41.36
Total	150	42	108	137.10	29.10	19.40
		Unit bet on home team "benchmark"				
2006–07	300	143	157	169.83	12.83	4.28
2007–08	326	150	176	159.38	−16.62	−5.10
2008–09	226	92	134	111.62	−22.38	−9.90
2009–10	271	134	137	161.80	24.80	9.15
2010–11	282	131	151	160.15	9.15	3.24
2011–12	264	124	140	141.22	1.22	0.46
Total	1669	774	895	904.00	9.00	0.54

The bottom panel of Table 4 shows a benchmark set of returns from betting on home teams. In some seasons, betting purely on home teams would have generated a profit (4.3% in 2006/07 and 9.1% in 2009/10) but returns are volatile across seasons the average return over the whole sample is negligible at +0.54%. In every season, the Fink Tank predictions generate higher returns from backing home teams where expected returns are positive compared to a naive strategy of just backing home teams.

Of course a one unit bet on every outcome where expected return is positive does not make allowance for either the magnitude of the expected return or the probability of occurrence. A standard staking system in the betting literature is to employ the variable Kelly stake as a proportion of wealth as a solution to this problem. See Sung and Johnson [20,21] for applications of Kelly investment strategies to the horse race betting market.

The Kelly stake is the optimal stake for an expected utility maximiser who has a logarithmic utility function. Expected utility, *Eu*, is given by

$$Eu = p \log(w + sO) + (1 - p) \log(w - s) \tag{2}$$

where w is the agent's betting wealth, s is the stake, O are odds and *p* is the probability of winning. Differentiating (1) with respect to s we obtain the optimal stake as

$$\frac{s}{w} = \frac{\mu}{O} = \frac{pO - (1-p)}{O} \tag{3}$$

Our second betting strategy, is to determine returns based on staking $s = \mu/o$ on each match where μ is positive and assuming betting wealth is fixed at $w = 1$. The returns are reported in Table 5. The important point to note from Table 5 is that actual returns to betting homes matches where expected returns are positive generates a positive return in each season with an average return of 10.53%. Actual returns to betting on away wins or draws were both negative.

Table 5. Returns on home, away and draw bets when using Kelly single stake.

Season	Winning bets	Losing bets	Winning stakes	Losing stakes	Wins	Profit	Return (%)
			Home				
2006–07	65	67	82.95	82.95	88.36	5.41	3.26
2007–08	63	80	64.81	63.07	69.98	6.91	5.40
2008–09	53	69	58.84	45.26	63.25	17.99	17.28
2009–10	68	83	76.66	73.18	93.93	20.75	13.85
2010–11	74	76	92.43	74.01	94.16	20.15	12.11
2011–12	61	73	58.05	60.69	77.18	16.49	13.89
Total	384	448	433.74	399.17	486.86	87.69	10.53
			Away				
2006–07	31	99	35.91	79.35	79.97	0.62	0.54
2007–08	47	142	33.55	83.63	55.55	−28.08	−23.96
2008–09	44	89	36.73	53.21	76.37	23.17	25.76
2009–10	27	118	14.36	79.73	33.55	−46.18	−49.08
2010–11	34	127	32.38	97.85	104.64	6.8	5.22
2011–12	39	126	26.66	78.17	74.68	−3.48	−3.32
Total	222	701	179.58	471.93	424.77	−47.15	−7.24
			Draw				
2006–07	12	29	3.81	13.96	11.92	−2.04	−11.48
2007–08	8	11	1.09	1.56	6.03	4.46	168.30
2008–09	3	9	0.26	1.57	0.80	−0.770	−42.08
2009–10	3	22	1.58	14.14	4.34	−9.80	−62.34
2010–11	6	14	1.39	3.17	4.01	0.84	18.42
2011–12	10	23	1.47	3.66	6.06	2.40	46.78
Total	42	108	9.61	38.06	33.15	−4.91	−10.30

If we examine the actual proportions of home away and draws outcomes and the proportions predicted obtained from best bookmaker odds and the Fink Tank we observe in Table 6 that the average of the Fink Tank probability exactly matched the proportion of outcomes but was too high and too low for away wins and draws respectively.

Table 6. Actual Proportions of Outcomes and Predicted based on best bookmaker's odds (BM) and Fink Tank (FT).

	Home win	Home probability (BM)	Home probability (FT)
N	1669	1669	1669
Mean	0.464	0.452	0.464
St. dev.	0.499	0.183	0.185
Minimum	0.000	0.052	0.040
Maximum	1.000	0.869	0.930
	Away win	Away probability (BM)	Away probability (FT)
N	1669	1669	1669
Mean	0.268	0.289	0.305
St. dev.	0.443	0.163	0.162
Minimum	0.000	0.033	0.020
Maximum	1.000	0.824	0.850
	Draw	Draw probability (BM)	Draw probability (FT)
N	1669	1669	1669
Mean	0.268	0.259	0.231
St. dev.	0.443	0.045	0.049
Minimum	0.000	0.097	0.030
Maximum	1.000	0.315	0.730

Of course punters may not be expected utility maximizers with a logarithmic utility function or may be non-expected utility maximizers. They could, for example, be better described as expected utility maximizers with a power or exponential utility function or non-expected utility maximizers of either Tversky and Kahneman's cumulative prospect theory [22] or Markowitz [23]. We therefore computed returns for a variety of alternative expected utility or non-expected value functions. The results were qualitatively similar to those reported for stakes based on the Kelly ratio. For example, in Table 7 we report the returns from betting on home teams with positive expected values for an expected utility maximiser with an exponential utility function as follows:

$$U = 1 - e^{-rw}, s = \frac{\log\left[\frac{(1+\mu)O}{O-\mu}\right]}{r(1+O)} \tag{4}$$

The parameter r cancels in computation of actual returns.

The actual returns in Table 4, Table 5, Table 7, and Table 8 were computed employing the best odds from 10 bookmakers. In Table 8, we report the returns if agents bet solely with William Hill or Ladbrokes when expected returns were positive employing the Kelly ratio. We observe by comparing Tables 5 and 8 that the average return to betting on home wins is some 4% lower, while returns are negative in the season 2006–07 (−4.19%) but positive for this season (3.26%) across the 10 bookmakers. Clearly, choosing bets from more bookmaker accounts will increase returns, ceteris paribus and without considering transactions costs of choices.

Formal evidence of the incremental value in the Fink Tank prediction of home win outcomes but not away wins or draws relative to the probability based on the best bookmaker odds is shown by the probit regressions reported in Table 9. Our analysis shows that a betting strategy based on the Fink Tank probabilities of home wins would have generated positive expected returns in the last six seasons of Premier League matches. It is clear that betting at the best odds on matchday would increase expected returns by perhaps 2%–3% at the cost of having a greater number of bookmaker accounts. Overall, our results provide a striking example of semi-strong inefficiency.

Table 7. Constant Absolute Risk Aversion.

Season	Winning bets	Losing bets	Winning stakes	Losing stakes	Wins	Profit	Return (%)
2006–07	66	67	85.12	85.23	85.60	0.37	0.22
2007–08	65	78	68.50	60.82	70.23	9.42	7.28
2008–09	53	70	61.30	44.66	62.63	17.97	16.96
2009–10	68	83	76.81	69.73	89.97	20.23	13.81
2010–11	73	77	102.53	73.81	97.38	23.57	13.37
2011–12	61	72	56.80	56.33	73.58	17.25	15.25
Total	386	447	451.07	390.58	479.39	88.81	10.55

The Fink Tank predictions are now available online during the week preceding a match. As a consequence, this will enable a bettor employing the Fink Tank home predictions far more opportunities to bet on home wins with positive expected value as the different bookmakers odds change over the course of the week. The adjustment of betting odds on football matches by bookmakers up to kick-off is a relatively recent phenomenon in the UK. Forrest [24] records how bookmakers in the 1990s and early 2000s used to keep odds fixed and stationary in the two or three days before a match. Such a position became untenable with the emergence of internet betting combined with increased global competition in betting markets. Of course, if bettors who were able to stake between them relatively large amounts were to employ the Fink Tank predictions, with consequent systematic and persistent returns, then at some point the bookmakers would have to set odds that reflected more closely the predictions of Fink Tank.

Table 8. Returns on home, away and draw bets using Kelly stake with Ladbrokes or William Hill when expected returns is positive.

Season	Winning bets	Losing bets	Winning stakes	Losing stakes	Wins	Profit	Return (%)
			Home				
2006–07	52	55	62.10	64.14	58.85	−5.29	−4.19
2007–08	49	50	41.01	37.46	37.66	0.20	0.25
2008–09	44	62	44.52	36.59	46.93	10.34	12.75
2009–10	57	80	61.28	62.32	76.99	14.67	11.87
2010–11	65	65	81.85	64.29	78.29	14.01	9.59
2011–12	57	67	50.50	53.11	62.26	9.15	8.83
Total	324	379	341.25	317.91	360.98	43.08	6.54
			Away				
2006–07	28	75	27.34	58.88	55.52	−3.35	−3.89
2007–08	31	74	19.76	44.83	28.32	−16.50	−25.55
2008–09	35	72	29.18	39.87	54.92	15.05	21.80
2009–10	22	108	11.20	67.61	25.79	−41.82	−53.06
2010–11	32	112	27.63	79.82	83.78	3.96	3.69
2011–12	35	116	21.61	63.62	52.94	−10.69	−12.54
Total	183	557	136.73	354.63	301.27	−53.36	−10.86
			Draw				
2006–07	6	14	1.21	9.03	3.11	−5.91	−57.71
2007–08	1	1	0.51	0.90	3.60	2.70	191.49
2008–09	1	5	0.10	0.78	0.35	−0.43	−48.86
2009–10	3	17	1.48	12.72	3.90	−8.82	−62.11
2010–11	5	9	1.27	1.76	3.67	1.91	63.04
2011–12	3	8	0.65	0.87	2.67	1.80	118.42
Total	19	54	5.23	26.06	17.31	−8.75	−27.96

3. Apparent Pure Arbitrage Possibilities

In our analysis we employed the best odds from 10 bookmakers available to us over our sample period. The website [25] supplied the odds for 18 bookmakers and two betting exchanges. The website highlights the best home, draw and away odds available and the over round based on these odds. The over round is the sum of probability implied by the odds. This sum is typically greater than unity but on rare occasions can be below unity which would indicate the potential for a pure arbitrage gain.

Bookmakers quote odds that are fixed for the bettor at the time of placing the wager. This means that the terms of the bettor's wager are unaltered before the finish of the match. Significant changes in the bookmakers' quoted odds tend to occur frequently from the first listing of odds, about three weeks before the match until the end of the match. The odds will change over the betting period in response to a number of factors. These include protection against insider trading activity [26] and public news about fundamentals such as player injuries [27]. Bookmakers will change their subjective probability of match outcomes as they attempt to maximize their objective function. This could involve deliberately setting the "wrong" prices on some outcomes to exploit sentiment or as "loss leaders" [7,15].

Table 9. Probit models with marginal effects for home win, away win and draw.

Home win			
	(1)	(2)	(3)
Home probability (BM)	1.060 ***		0.571 ***
	(14.460)		(3.043)
Home probability (FT)		1.043 ***	0.523 ***
		(14.350)	(2.807)
Observations	1669	1669	1669
Pseudo R^2	0.097	0.096	0.100
Away win			
	(4)	(5)	(6)
Away probability (BM)	1.006 ***		0.873 ***
	(15.078)		(5.284)
Away probability (FT)		0.955 ***	0.146
		(14.210)	(0.872)
Observations	1669	1669	1669
Pseudo R^2	0.121	0.106	0.121
Draw			
	(7)	(8)	(9)
Draw probability (BM)	1.144 ***		0.979 ***
	(4.484)		(2.660)
Draw probability (FT)		0.836 ***	0.201
		(3.576)	(0.627)
Observations	1669	1669	1669
Pseudo R^2	0.010	0.007	0.011

BM—Best bookmaker's odds, FT—Fink Tank; *** denotes significance at 1 percent.

The over round for a particular bookmaker and the over round employing the best odds across bookmakers, from the punters perspective, each tends to fall as match day approaches. The over round of an individual bookmaker on a given match at kick-off is always above unity at approximately 8% (1.08). Previous studies have reported over rounds of around 10% to 12% [23] and the lower current figure is most likely a consequence of competition from betting exchanges such as Betfair [28]. The over round across bookmakers is typically around 1 to 2% (1.01 to 1.02). In the week leading up to kick off, it is not unusual to observe an over round less than unity in up to three Premier League matches per day, with a few others in lower divisions, based on the best odds of typically three to four out of 20 bookmakers. The identities of bookmakers involved in these apparent pure arbitrage possibilities vary from day to day.

The possibility of pure arbitrage profits was identified in a number of earlier papers and has clearly not disappeared over two decades since first noted by Pope and Peel [2]. However, we are highly quizzical about whether pure arbitrage profits of any economically significant amount can be systematically realized. It is possible that bookmakers are unaware when the over round across bookmakers becomes negative, as a necessary condition for pure arbitrage, but we doubt this if only because of the existence of internet comparison sites such as Betrescue [25], which has direct links to all bookmakers quoted in our sample, together with the apparent existence of such pure arbitrage bets since at least 1989.

An over round of below unity is necessary, but not sufficient, for a pure arbitrage opportunity. There are direct costs associated with undertaking an arbitrage. An arbitrage will not be riskless. In order to undertake arbitrage bets, it will be necessary for the bettor to have funds deposited in a number of bookmaker accounts since inspection suggests that arbitrage possibilities are not concentrated across a few bookmakers. Clearly, the less the number of bookmaker accounts covered the fewer the arbitrage opportunities available. It appears that at least 10 accounts would be needed to achieve a reasonable number of arbitrage possibilities. An arbitrage gain of £10 would appear to require an outlay typically of £500 or more so a large capital base is required. Also, there are costs and delays in depositing and withdrawing funds. While specialist methods for fund transfers do exist, such as eWallets, withdrawals are often limited to a particular amount per month or to a specific number of free monthly withdrawals. Withdrawals tend to be charged for on the eWallet side. For many bettors with medium sized stakes, these transactions costs could amount to 2% to 3% of the stake which would wipe out positive returns from arbitrage trades. For very large traders, the very existence of their accounts with large deposits and withdrawals draw the attention of bookmakers to arbitrage attempts. Bookmakers can then suddenly suspend bettor accounts imposing potentially large losses on the arbitrageur.

The formulae for the stakes on the home, *ho*, draw, *dr*, and away, *aw*, to obtain a pure arbitrage gain of 1 when the over round across bookmakers is less than one and the home odds are *a*, draw odds, *b*, and away odds, *c*, are given by

$$ho = \frac{1 + b + c + bc}{abc - a - b - c - 2} \tag{5}$$

$$dr = \frac{1 + a + c + ac}{abc - a - b - c - 2} \tag{6}$$

$$aw = \frac{1 + a + b + ab}{abc - a - b - c - 2} \tag{7}$$

A necessary condition for a pure arbitrage gain is that $abc - a - b - c - 2 > 0$. If one of the outcomes is heavily odds on the amounts required to be bet to earn one unit can be relatively large. For example the pure arbitrage odds $a = 1/5$, $b = 17/2$ and $c = 18/1$ (Manchester City *versus* Southampton opening day of the 2012/13 Premier League season) required a total bet of £113 to win one £1. (*home* = £95, *draw* = £12, *away* = £6). Consequently, large outlays would typically be needed to generate an arbitrage paper gain of £10. Our estimate is typically around is £500. As noted above, if the arbitrageur's capital base is large enough this profit can be realized but a bookmaker can impose maximum limits on the size of a stake without warning, leaving the arbitrageur with costs as she attempts to cover the bet with other bookmakers.

Overall, it seems scarcely credible that bookmakers are unaware of arbitrage opportunities given that they are linked to comparison web sites such as Betrescue [25]. Bookmakers have expressed a dim view of arbitrage attempts. They can close accounts or refuse bets without warning and thus potentially impose substantial costs on arbitrageurs as they remove the arbitrage possibility after some of the components have been bet. We should add that the odds can also change for fundamental reasons so that the arbitrage opportunity disappears after one or two components of the arbitrage bet have been placed.

Case Studies of Pure Arbitrage

We followed an apparent arbitrage possibility through from their first appearance on Betrescue [25] to their removal. The typical pattern is shown by the following two examples of arbitrage opportunity. On Monday October 1st 2012 at 6:40 p.m. the best odds for the forthcoming Swansea *versus* Reading match on October 6th included 1/1 for the home win (quoted by three of 19 bookmakers on Betrescue [25], namely Stan James, BLUESQ, and Boyesports). The best draw odds were quoted by BETVICTOR at 29/10. The best away odds were quoted by BETVICTOR and Panbet at 7/2. For this match it would be necessary to stake a total of £45.8 to obtain a £1 gain. (*home* = £23.4, *draw* = £12, *away* = £10.4). We noted that bookmaker BETVICTOR was posting the worst odds on

Int. J. Financial Stud. **2013**, *1*, 168–182

the home at this time but the best odds available for the draw and away. On Tuesday at 10am this arbitrage possibility had disappeared with a new over round of 1.008. The best home odds of 1/1 were still being quoted by Stan James and BLUESQ. Boyesports and BETVICTOR were quoting 23/10 the draw, (the best draw odds were 13/5 with 32RED, BET365 or bodog). The best away odds were now 10/3 quoted by Panbet.

West Bromwich Albion *versus* Queens Park Rangers, to be played on October 12th 2012 also offered a pure arbitrage possibility again on Monday October 1st 2012 at 6.40 p.m. 21/20 (home win) quoted by Stan James, 11/4 (draw) quoted by 32RED, BETVICTOR and Bodog and 7/2 (away) quoted by Panbet. £42 stake was required to win £1 *i.e.*, home win bet of £20.93, draw bet of £11.44 and away win bet of £9.53 with an over round of 0.977. Note that the draw odds in this arbitrage example were the same on Tuesday at 11.40 am as on Monday at 6 40 pm, the previous day. However, by Tuesday at 12.10 pm this arbitrage opportunity had gone. Best odds were now 19/20 home win (Skybet), 11/4/ draw (32RED) and 10/3 away win (Panbet) giving an over round of 1.01.

Clearly, these arbitrage possibilities could have disappeared due to pure arbitrage dealing staggered over time. Arbitrage opportunities signalled by a below-unity over round may fall under the heading of 'limits to arbitrage' proposed by Shleifer and Vishny [29] who suggested that arbitrage possibilities may not quickly disappear. Alternatively, Kondor [30] developed a model of competition between arbitrageurs in standard asset markets. An arbitrageur faces the risk that the opportunity may disappear as she tries to exploit it. The arbitrageur may leave the opportunity 'on the table' in order to exploit future (more lucrative) arbitrage possibilities.

In our examples, the arbitrage possibilities did not disappear quickly. Most money has to be wagered on the favourite in a pure arbitrage bet, In the Swansea-Reading match the odds for the home outcome of the three bookmakers offering the best home odds were unchanged at 1/1. This is suggestive of a persistent arbitrage opportunity. Rather, some bettors appear to have bet on draw and away win outcomes at the more favourable odds. Similarly, in the West Bromwich Albion-Queens Park Rangers match the draw odds remained unchanged over the duration of the arbitrage possibility.

4. Conclusions

Previous literature has reported some evidence of inefficiency in bookmakers' pricing of odds in fixed odds betting, including the potential for pure arbitrage gains betting with different bookmakers. In this paper we add to this literature and report striking evidence that betting on the Fink Tank probability of home wins across 10 bookmakers when there are positive expected returns, would have generated positive returns in each of the seasons from 2006–07 to 2011–12 for a variety of different betting strategies. These returns could have been enhanced by employing the best odds from a greater number of bookmakers. The inefficiency associated with Fink Tank match outcome probability is unlikely to be due to systematic mistakes. Bookmakers will change their subjective probability of match outcomes as they attempt to maximize their objective function. This could involve deliberately setting the "wrong" prices on some outcomes to exploit sentiment or as "loss leaders". The extent to which the inefficiencies derived here from Fink Tank probability can be attributed to either or both of these sources of mispricing is a useful topic for further research.

We noted that paper pure arbitrage opportunities occur quite frequently, perhaps a handful a day, as bookmakers change odds in response to betting flows and news or possibly in an attempt to induce betting flows. The fact that these pure arbitrage bets have existed for years and appear to last for several hours or even days suggest they are in practice not exploitable to a magnitude that poses any threat to bookmakers. Similar remarks apply to betting strategies based on the Fink Tank probability of home win.

Bookmakers appear to set prices that are informationally (semi-strong) inefficient. However, the degree of inefficiency has clearly not been exploited to date on a scale that presents a probability problem for bookmakers. The transactions costs and risks attached to trading on the mispricing,

Int. J. Financial Stud. **2013**, *1*, 168–182

revealed by Fink Tank probability and from other sources, appear to insulate bookmakers to a large degree from arbitrageurs.

Acknowledgments: The authors thank participants at the 2012 Gijon conference on sports economics for helpful comments.

Conflicts of Interest: The authors declare no conflict of interest.

References

1. Thaler, R.H.; Ziemba, W.T. Anomalies Parimutuel Betting Markets: Racetracks and Lotteries. *J. Econ. Pers.* **1988**, *2*, 161–174. [CrossRef]
2. Pope, P.F.; Peel, D.A. Information, Prices and Efficiency in a Fixed-Odds Betting Market. *Economica* **1989**, *56*, 323–341. [CrossRef]
3. Cain, M.; Law, D.; Peel, D.A. Testing for Statistical and Market Efficiency When Forecast Errors Are Non-Normal: The NFL Betting Market Revisited. *J. Forecast.* **2000**, *19*, 575–586. [CrossRef]
4. Constantinou, A.C.; Fenton, N.E. Solving the Problem of Inadequate Scoring Rules for Assessing Probabilistic Football Forecast Models. *J. Quant. Anal. Sports* **2012**, *8*. [CrossRef]
5. Forrest, D.; Simmons, R. Forecasting Sport: The Behaviour and Performance of Football Tipsters. *Int. J. Forecast.* **2000**, *16*, 317–331. [CrossRef]
6. Franck, E.; Verbeek, E.; Nüesch, S. Prediction Accuracy of Different Market Structures: Bookmakers versus a Betting Exchange. *Int. J. Forecast.* **2010**, *26*, 448–459. [CrossRef]
7. Franck, E.; Verbeek, E.; Nüesch, S. Sentimental Preferences and the Organizational Regime of Betting Markets. *South. Econ. J.* **2011**, *78*, 502–518. [CrossRef]
8. Goddard, J.; Asimakopoulos, I. Forecasting Football Results and the Efficiency of Fixed-odds Betting. *J. Forecast.* **2004**, *23*, 51–66. [CrossRef]
9. Vlastakis, N.; Dotsis, G.; Markellos, R.N. How Efficient Is the European Football Betting Market? Evidence from Arbitrage and Trading Strategies. *J. Forecast.* **2009**, *28*, 426–444. [CrossRef]
10. Sauer, R.D. The Economics of Wagering Markets. *J. Econ. Lit.* **1998**, *36*, 2021–2064.
11. Williams, L.V. Information Efficiency in Betting Markets: A Survey. *Bull. Econ. Res.* **1999**, *51*, 1–39.
12. Levitt, S.D. Why Are Gambling Markets Organised So Differently From Financial Markets? *Econ. J.* **2004**, *114*, 223–246. [CrossRef]
13. Humphreys, B.R. The Financial Consequences of Unbalanced Betting on NFL Games. *Int. J. Sport Financ.* **2011**, *6*, 60–71.
14. Paul, R.J.; Weinbach, A.P. Does Sportsbook.com Set Pointspreads to Maximize Profits? Tests of the Levitt Model of Sportsbook Behavior. *J. Pred. Markets* **2007**, *1*, 209–218.
15. Forrest, D.; Simmons, R. Sentiment in the Betting Market on Spanish Football. *Appl. Econ.* **2008**, *40*, 119–126. [CrossRef]
16. The Fink Tank Predictor. Available online: www.dectech.co.uk/football_sites/football (accessed on 12 November 2013).
17. Constantinou, A.C.; Fenton, N.E. Profiting From Arbitrage and Odds Biases of the European Football Gambling Market. *J. Gambl. Bus. Econ.* **2013**, *7*, 41–70.
18. Graham, I.; Stott, H. Predicting Bookmaker Odds and Efficiency for UK Football. *Appl. Econ.* **2008**, *40*, 99–109. [CrossRef]
19. Forrest, D.; Goddard, J.; Simmons, R. Odds-Setters as Forecasters: The Case of English Football. *Int. J. Forecast.* **2005**, *21*, 551–564. [CrossRef]
20. Sung, M.; Johnson, J.E.V. Revealing Weak-Form Inefficiency in a Market for State Contingent Claims: The Importance of Market Ecology, Modelling Procedures and Investment Strategies. *Economica* **2010**, *77*, 128–147. [CrossRef]
21. Sung, M.C.; Johnson, J.E.V.; Peirson, J. Discovering a Profitable Trading Strategy in an Apparently Efficient Market: Exploiting the Actions of Less Informed Traders in Speculative Markets. *J. Bus. Financ. Acc.* **2012**, *39*, 1131–1159.
22. Tversky, A.; Kahneman, D. Advances in Prospect Theory: Cumulative Representation of Uncertainty. *J. Risk Uncertain.* **1992**, *5*, 297–323. [CrossRef]

23. Markowitz, H. The Utility of Wealth. *J. Polit. Econ.* **1952**, *60*, 151–158.
24. Forrest, D. Soccer Betting in Britain. In *Handbook of Sports and Lottery Markets*; Hausch, D., Ziemba, W., Eds.; Elsevier: Amsterdam, The Netherlands, 2008; pp. 421–446.
25. Bet Rescue. Available online: www.betrescue.com (accessed on 12 November 2013).
26. Shin, H.S. Prices of State Contingent Claims With Insider Traders, and the Favourite-Longshot Bias. *Econ. J.* **1992**, *102*, 426–435. [CrossRef]
27. Makropoulou, V.; Markellos, R.N. Optimal Price Setting in Fixed-Odds Betting Markets under Information Uncertainty. *Scot. J. Polit. Econ.* **2011**, *58*, 519–536. [CrossRef]
28. Franck, E.; Verbeek, E.; Nüesch, S. Inter-market Arbitrage in Betting. *Economica* **2013**, *80*, 302–325.
29. Shleifer, A.; Vishny, R.W. The Limits of Arbitrage. *J. Financ.* **1997**, *52*, 35–55. [CrossRef]
30. Kondor, P. Risk in Dynamic Arbitrage: The Price Effects of Convergence Trading. *J. Financ.* **2009**, *64*, 631–655. [CrossRef]

International Journal of
Financial Studies

MDPI

Article

Market Efficiency and Behavioral Biases in the WNBA Betting Market

Rodney J. Paul [1,]* and Andrew P. Weinbach [2]

[1] Department of Sport Management, David B. Falk College of Sport and Human Dynamics, Syracuse University, 810 Nottingham Road, Syracuse, NY 13224-8165, USA

[2] E. Craig Wall Sr. College of Business Administration, Coastal Carolina University, P.O. Box 261954, Conway, SC 26195, USA; aweinbac@coastal.edu

* Author to whom correspondence should be addressed; rpaul01@syr.edu; Tel.: +1-585-748-5092; Fax: +1-315-443-9716.

Received: 24 February 2014; in revised form: 9 April 2014; Accepted: 14 April 2014; Published: 24 April 2014

Abstract: The betting market for the Women's National Basketball Association (WNBA) is a thin financial market, which does not attract much interest from sports bettors. Given these characteristics, it is possible that profitable wagering strategies could exist for informed bettors of the WNBA. Using betting data on the WNBA from 2007–2012, we find that simple betting strategies do not earn statistically significant returns. WNBA bettors are like NBA bettors; however, in that they strongly prefer the best teams, particularly when they are on the road. Despite this clear bias, betting against the most popular public wagers is not found to earn statistically significant profits.

Keywords: efficient markets; gambling; behavioral biases

JEL Classification: G14; G10; G02

1. Introduction

Most of the betting on professional basketball in the United States is tied to National Basketball Association (NBA) games, the dominant men's league which offers the greatest exposure and highest salaries in the world of basketball. Women's basketball also has a professional league in North America, the WNBA. A wagering market also exists for the WNBA, but the betting market for the WNBA is quite small and attracts little interest relative to the NBA. According to records of data from [1], for participating sportsbooks, the average betting volume for a WNBA game is under 1200 bets per game, which is extremely small compared to the average betting volume in men's professional and college sports. In comparison, NBA games attracted roughly 10,000 bets per game during the same period. In terms of dollars bet, although [1] does not directly provide this information, Humphreys *et al.* [2] obtained dollars bet from an online sportsbook and found that the [1] information on the number of bets are highly correlated with the dollars bet on a game (correlation coefficient of 0.85).

Given the thin nature of this betting market and the apparent general lack of interest it generates among most male bettors, it is possible that profitable opportunities may exist in betting the WNBA which would not exist in betting the NBA or other mainstream sports. The nature of the thin market may make it exploitable if sports book managers do not spend the resources to update their information on teams and players. The possibility of market inefficiencies existing in thin betting markets has been explored in horse and dog racing (*i.e.*, Gramm and Owens [3] and Weinbach and Paul [4]). A thin betting market where market efficiency was rejected in team sports was found for the Arena Football League (Borghesi *et al.* [5]), where betting volume is quite low compared to other North American sports.

Int. J. Financial Stud. **2014**, *2*, 193–202

If informed bettors do exist within the WNBA betting market, it may be possible to determine their existence through tests for market efficiency and unbiasedness and betting simulations based on simple wagering strategies. If the sports book sets point spreads that are accurate, however, these profitable opportunities may not exist even within the context of this thin market.

To examine this betting market, we obtained WNBA betting data from [1] for the 2007–2012 seasons. The data obtained from [1] not only includes the standard pointspread and game outcome information, but it also includes information on betting percentages. The betting percentages note the percentage of the betting action on favorites and underdogs in this market.

Levitt [6] used data from a betting tournament to illustrate that sportsbooks do not adhere to the balanced book hypothesis. In his study of the NFL, Levitt [6] showed that bettors prefer favorites (in particular road favorites) in that more bets accrue on favorites, and the sportsbook appears to allow unbalanced betting action to maximize profits. Paul and Weinbach [7,8] used data from actual on-line sportsbooks and similarly reject the balanced book hypothesis for the NFL and the NBA. The difference between the NFL and NBA betting markets is that in the NFL, the sportsbook appears to shade the pointspread toward the favorite using their knowledge of the biases of the betting public to earn additional profits. In the NBA, however, the sportsbook does not appear to shade the pointspread, even in the presence of significant imbalances, but appears to price more as a forecast of game outcomes. This difference is likely due to the larger volume of betting which occurs in the NFL compared to the NBA, where sportsbooks may have a greater incentive to undertake the transactions costs to shade the point spread in NFL games compared to NBA games (Paul and Weinbach [8]).

Given the relatively smaller size of the WNBA betting market, does the WNBA market work in the same fashion as the NBA betting market? To examine this question and to explore if there is any evidence of informed betting actions by the wagering public, we explore a few avenues with the gambling data available through [1]. First, we run a simple test for market efficiency based on a regression model of pointspreads and game outcomes. Then, we test if big underdogs and home underdogs win more than implied by efficiency through simple betting simulations. In the NBA, big underdogs and home underdogs were shown to outperform favorites (Paul and Weinbach [8]) as the null hypothesis of a fair bet (win percentage is equal to 50%) could be rejected but the null hypothesis of no profitability (win percentage is equal to 52.4%—the percentage needed to break even given the bet $11 to win $10 rule in sports wagering) could not be rejected.

We then use the WNBA betting percentage data to test the null hypothesis of a balanced book (equal betting action on both sides of the wagering proposition). After examining this relationship with respect to the size of the favorite based on the pointspread and a road favorite dummy variable, we explore simple betting simulations based upon wagering with or against the public when a certain threshold of bets accrue on the favorite (*i.e.*, 70% or more, 60% or more, *etc.*). We compare these results to the research performed on the NBA betting market and conclude the paper with some thoughts as to the similarities and differences between these basketball betting markets.

2. Market Efficiency Tests and Betting Simulations—WNBA

To begin our analysis, we will test the WNBA betting market under the null hypothesis of market efficiency using standard regression analysis outlined in Zuber *et al.* [9] and Sauer *et al.* [10]. Data for the WNBA gambling market was purchased from [1], a website specializing in sports gambling information. The years included in our sample are 2007 through 2012. Games for which no betting action was reported, or in cases where pertinent information was missing, were removed from the sample. Summary statistics for games with home favorites and games with road favorites are shown in the summary statistics below (Table 1).

Table 1. Summary Statistics for Women's National Basketball Association (WNBA) Home and Road Favorites 2007–2012.

	Home Favorites	*Observations = 978*	
	Pointspread	Score Differential	% Bet on Favorite
Mean	5.98	5.25	53.50
Median	5.50	6.00	54.00
Standard Deviation	3.26	11.58	15.29
	Road Favorites	*Observations = 305*	
	Pointspread	Score Differential	% Bet on Favorite
Mean	4.71	3.85	68.09
Median	4.00	6.00	69.00
Standard Deviation	2.91	12.55	12.33

The basic regression model to test market efficiency in this simple financial betting market takes the form:

$$\text{Score} = \alpha_0 + \beta_1 \text{ Line} + \varepsilon_1 \tag{1}$$

Score is the scoring differential between the favorite team and the underdog team, Line is the pointspread on the game, and ε_1 is the error term with its normal properties. To test for market efficiency, the joint hypothesis is tested that $\alpha_0 = 0$ and $\beta_1 = 1$. Results are presented in Table 2 below.

Using a simple regression-based test, market efficiency in the WNBA betting market is rejected at the 10% level. The f-test that the intercept is equal to zero and the coefficient on the pointspread is equal to one takes a value of 2.82 and rejects market efficiency at the 10% threshold. Although the basic test for market efficiency is rejected, this does not imply that profitable wagering strategies exist. Further tests are necessary to examine if this market offers potential positive betting market returns.

Table 2. Regression Results—Efficiency Test—WNBA. Dependent Variable: Score Differential (Favorite Score—Underdog Score).

Variable	Coefficient
	(T-Statistic)
Intercept	−1.01 (−1.59)
Pointspread	1.05 *** (10.72)
F-Test—Intercept = 0 and Pointspread = 1	F-statistic (Probability Value) 2.82 (0.06)

***: statistical significance of the t-test at the 1% level.

To test for possible profitable betting strategies in the WNBA, we use a simple betting simulation, observing the win-loss record of favorites and underdogs during our sample of the 2007 through 2012 seasons. We break the sample into home and road favorites, due to previous findings of successful wagering strategies based on betting on home underdogs. Research on betting markets have found profitability in wagering on home underdogs in the NFL in studies by Dare and McDonald [11], Golec and Tamarkin [12], and Dare and Holland [13] with similar findings in the NBA in studies such as Paul and Weinbach [8]. It appears across sports using point spreads that there is the tendency for bettors to underestimate the home field advantage of inferior teams (or overestimate the abilitiesof the superior road teams), which could help to explain the favorable results found in wagering on home underdogs.

We choose various thresholds of favorites, denoting big favorites where there is a large enough sample of games to yield potentially meaningful inferences. For home favorites, we present the results for favorites of 10 points or more, 9 points or more, *etc.* and for the overall sample of home favorites (all). For road favorites, where the implicit home court advantage leads to fewer large road favorites, we choose thresholds of 7 points or more, 6 points or more, *etc.* and for the overall sample of road favorites (all).

Results related to home favorites are presented in Table 3 and road favorites are presented in Table 4. In each table, favorite wins, underdog wins, pushes (game outcome equals pointspread), win percentage, and log likelihood ratio tests for a fair bet (win percentage equal 0.500) and for no profits (win percentage equal 0.524) are presented. The null of a fair bet is a test for unbiasedness of the pointspread. The null of no profits tests if any bias in the pointspread is exploitable compared to transactions costs within the market (overcoming the bookmaker commission).

The log likelihood test statistics have a chi-square distribution with one degree of freedom. Critical Values are 2.70 (for an $\alpha = 0.10$), 3.84 (for an $\alpha = 0.05$), and 6.64 (for an $\alpha = 0.01$).

Table 3. Betting Simulation Results—WNBA—Home Favorites.

Pointspread greater than or equal to:	Favorite Wins	Underdog Wins	Pushes	Underdog Win Percentage	Log Likelihood Ratio Fair Bet	Log Likelihood Ratio No Profits
10	51	60	2	54.05%	0.73	0.12
9	74	85	2	53.46%	0.76	0.08
8	109	121	4	52.61%	0.63	0.00
7	156	180	5	53.57%	1.72	0.19
6	219	231	7	51.33%	0.32	NA
5	289	300	8	50.93%	0.21	NA
ALL	491	472	15	49.01%	0.37	NA

Table 4. Betting Simulation Results—WNBA—Road Favorites.

Point spread greater than or equal to:	Favorite Wins	Underdog Wins	Pushes	Favorite Win Percentage	Log Likelihood Ratio Fair Bet	Log Likelihood Ratio No Profits
7	42	29	1	59.15%	2.39	1.32
6	55	41	2	57.29%	2.05	0.93
5	70	59	2	54.26%	0.94	0.18
4	82	78	4	51.25%	0.10	NA
3	99	97	4	50.51%	0.02	NA
ALL	155	145	5	51.67%	0.33	NA

The log likelihood test statistics have a chi-square distribution with one degree of freedom. Critical Values are 2.7 (for an $\alpha = 0.10$), 3.8 (for an $\alpha = 0.05$), and 6.6 (for an $\alpha = 0.01$).

With respect to home favorites, underdogs were found to win slightly less than 50% of the time in the overall sample. These results, however, were not found to be statistically different from 50% from the log likelihood ratio test. For big home favorites, road underdogs were found to win in excess of 53% at the various thresholds examined. The null hypothesis of a fair bet (and therefore the null hypothesis of no profitability) could not be rejected at normal significance levels. These results are similar to what was found for the NBA betting market in Paul and Weinbach [8] in that underdogs outperformed favorites, but returns were not great enough to earn statistically significant profits.

Table 3 presented the results for road favorites. In the case of road favorites, the favorite was shown to win more than 50% of the time overall, with some high win percentages at the highest thresholds observed. In all cases, however, the null hypothesis of a fair bet (and therefore also the null of no profitability) could not be rejected. These results are similar to the NBA (Paul and Weinbach [8]), where statistically significant results were not found in the sample of road favorites.

To test for robustness, we divided the sample in half and did the same tests for the games played early in the sample compared to late in the sample. Large road favorites (7+, 8+, and 9+ point favorites) did perform slightly better in the early part of our sample (2007–2009), rejecting the null hypothesis of a fair bet for these years. In the more recent sample (2010–2012), statistically significant results were not found. Therefore, there is some evidence that the simple strategy of wagering on the road underdogs has become less profitable over time. In relation to the sample of road favorites, no statistically significant results were found in either subsample.

Given that road favorites win more than 50% of the time in the WNBA, it is possible that the home court advantage is slightly overstated (although not statistically significant) in the WBNA betting market. Given that home field advantage incorporates a variety of factors in most sports (unique stadium attributes, being able to sleep at home rather than in a hotel, the intensity of the home crowd); the home field can be a potent factor. In the WNBA, however, home court may not be as pivotal as basketball courts are uniform in nature and small crowds for WNBA games may not affect opponents as much as lively sold-out arenas for sports such as the NBA. In any case, although favorites won more often than underdogs, the returns were not great enough to earn statistically significant results.

3. Betting Percentage Regression and Betting Simulation Results

In this section, we examine the determinants of betting percentages for the WNBA in the same manner they were examined for the NBA in Paul and Weinbach [8]. The source of our data, [1], reports the percentage of bets on the favoriteand the underdog. As noted in the introduction, however, Humphreys *et al.* [2] found that the dollars bet on a game are highly correlated with the number of bets reported by [1]. Therefore, the percentage of dollars bet on the game are highly correlated with the percentage of bets reported in our data set. A very simple regression model is tested, which illustrates the actions of the sportsbook. The model to be estimated is as follows for the sides (pointspread) market:

$$(\% \text{ Bet on the Favorite})_i = \alpha_0 + \beta_1(\text{Pointspread})_i + \beta_2(\text{Dummy for Road Favorite})_i + \varepsilon_i \qquad (2)$$

The dependent variable is the percentage of dollars bet on the favorite. The independent variables include an intercept, the pointspread on the game (presented as a positive number—greater favorites have larger pointspreads), and a dummy for teams which are road favorites. Road favorites have been shown to be commonly overbet in wagering market studies such as Golec and Tomarkin [12], Gray and Gray [14], and Levitt [6].

A couple of simple propositions can be tested from this regression model. First, if bettors overbet favorites and stronger favorites are bet more heavily than weaker favorites, the coefficient β_1 should be positive and significant. If bettors overbet road favorites, the coefficient on the dummy variable, β_2, should also be positive and significant. Under the balanced book hypothesis of sportsbook behavior, the intercept should be equal to 50 and the other coefficients should be equal to zero. The balanced book hypothesis has been rejected in similar studies for the NFL (Levitt [6]; Paul and Weinbach [7]), NBA (Paul and Weinbach [8]), College Basketball (Paul and Weinbach [15]) and other sports using data from [1] or similar data. Regression results are shown in Table 5 below.

As is the case for the NBA and other sports, the regression results for the WNBA soundly reject the null hypothesis of a balanced book. Although the intercept is found to be slightly under 50%, the percentage bet is found to increase with the magnitude of the favorite (by about three-quarters of a point for each point of the pointspread—significant at the 1% level) and road favorites are found to be heavily bet in this market, with an additional 15.5% bet on home favorites in this sample. In short, WNBA bettors, like bettors of other sports, appear to favor the best teams, particularly on the road.

Table 5. Regression Results—Determinants of Favorite Betting Percentage—WNBA. Dependent Variable: Percentage Bet on Favorite.

Variable	Coefficient (T-statistic)
Intercept	49.07 *** (55.02)
Pointspread	0.74 *** (5.81)
Road Favorite Dummy	15.56 *** (16.13)

***: statistical significance of the t-test at the 1% level.

To determine if the betting public finds a way to exploit the WNBA betting market, we run simple betting simulations observing results where one particular side of the betting proposition receives a disproportionate share of the betting action. We choose thresholds of 70% or more, 65% or more, 60% or more, and 55% or more for both home favorites (Table 6) and road favorites (Table 7). As with Tables 3 and 4 in the previous section, favorite wins, underdog wins, pushes, win percentage, and log likelihood ratio tests are presented. If the betting public can successfully pick winners, the more popular side of the proposition should win more than 50% of the time. In this scenario, the sportsbook would be losing money to bettors as the sportsbook is not balanced.

Table 6. Betting Simulations—Betting with the Public—Home Favorites.

Betting Percentage on Favorite greater than or equal to:	Favorite Wins	Underdog Wins	Pushes	Favorite Win Percentage	Log Likelihood Ratio Fair Bet	Log Likelihood Ratio No Profits
70	77	67	2	53.47%	0.70	0.07
65	110	106	2	50.93%	0.07	NA
60	167	160	3	51.07%	0.15	NA
55	247	226	5	52.22%	0.93	NA

The log likelihood test statistics have a chi-square distribution with one degree of freedom. Critical Values are 2.71 (for an $\alpha = 0.10$), 3.84 (for an $\alpha = 0.05$), and 6.63 (for an $\alpha = 0.01$).

Table 7. Betting Simulations—Betting with the Public—Road Favorites.

Betting Percentage on Favorite greater than or equal to:	Favorite Wins	Underdog Wins	Pushes	Favorite Win Percentage	Log Likelihood Ratio Fair Bet	Log Likelihood Ratio No Profits
70	74	70	2	51.39%	0.11	NA
65	101	86	4	54.01%	1.20	0.20
60	126	105	4	54.55%	1.91	0.44
55	135	123	5	52.33%	0.56	NA

The log likelihood test statistics have a chi-square distribution with one degree of freedom. Critical Values are 2.71 (for an $\alpha = 0.10$), 3.84 (for an $\alpha = 0.05$), and 6.64 (for an $\alpha = 0.01$).

For the sample of home favorites (Table 6), when the favorite is significantly overbet compared to the underdog, no statistical significance is found as the null of a fair bet (and no profitability) cannot be rejected. Win percentages are slightly above 50% in each threshold case studied. For the sample of road favorites (Table 7), win percentages are found to be slightly higher than for home favorites in the thresholds studied for relatively small samples (compared to home favorites). The null of a fair bet and the null of no profitability cannot be rejected in any of the groupings. As in the previous section, we also tested for robustness by dividing the sample in half for the market efficiency tests based upon unbalanced betting. Statistically significant results were not found in either subsample.

Unlike other sports, where either underdogs do slightly better than favorites when the favorites attract a high percentage of the betting action or the results are closer to an even 50/50 split, betting with popular road favorites in the WNBA wins more often than underdogs. If these results were to persist in a larger sample, it they could indicate the existence of some informed WNBA bettors, who are taking advantage of possible mispricing of the home court advantage in WNBA games. In this current sample, however, even though the percentages lean toward some inclination of informed bettors in this thinly-bet market, statistical significance cannot be found.

4. Conclusions

The betting market for the WNBA was examined both in terms of game outcomes compared to the pointspread and the preferences of the betting public, using betting percentages on favorites and underdogs. For the most part, the betting market for the WNBA is quite similar to other betting markets, with bettors exhibiting a tendency to wager on the better teams. This tendency to bet on the best teams is consistent with the idea that bettors are often fans, and betting on games may be viewed as a consumption activity, rather than strategic investment. Although market efficiency was rejected using the simple regression model approach, simple betting simulations did not reveal statistically significant results.

Studying the betting percentages on favorites and underdogs revealed a rejection of the balanced book hypothesis. Like other sports, the percentage bet on the favorite increases with each point of the pointspread by a statistically significant margin. In addition, road favorites attract a large (15%) and statistically significant increase in bets. Road favorites, however, were found to win more often than home underdogs. This is contrary to what is generally observed in other sports, where home underdogs have been shown to win more often than implied by efficiency and, in some cases, earn statistically significant profits (*i.e.*, Levitt [6], Paul and Weinbach [7]). Although favorites outperformed underdogs, statistically significant results were not found. The success of road favorites could reflect a possible overstating of home court advantage in the WNBA by sportsbooks, with smaller crowds at games providing less of an advantage.

With the relatively light volume and lower betting limits (limits of 10%–50% of NBA limits are common in the industry), it may also be the case that sportsbooks choose to invest fewer resources in setting and adjusting the lines in this market, or treat WNBA betting not as a money making proposition, but as a service offered to keep customers actively engaged in between seasons. Mayer [16] indicated that as an illegal bookie, he made little money on baseball betting, but provided it as a service to bettors to retain their loyalty and keep customers coming back for the football season. This type of behavior by the sportsbook could attract informed bettors into the market.

To determine if bettors of the WNBA are exploiting the sportsbook for profits, we performed some basic betting simulations based on different threshold levels of percentage bet on the favorite. When favorites, both home and road, attract a disproportionate share of the betting action, the null of a fair bet cannot be rejected with win percentages hovering around 50% for favorites and underdogs. One finding that was different from the NBA was that popular favorites outperformed their underdog opponents, as road favorites who received a disproportionate share of the betting activity won more than 50% of the time. As noted above, however, they did not win often enough to earn statistically significant returns.

Overall, the WNBA betting market appears similar to the betting market of the NBA, despite low overall bettor interest. Bettors of the WNBA prefer to bet on the best teams (big favorites), particularly when they are on the road. Even with the thin market and the biased views of bettors, simple betting strategies of wagering against the most popular public wagers did not win often enough to earn statistically significant profits. It appears book makers for the WNBA act in the same fashion as they do in other sports, essentially pricing as a function of expected game outcomes despite clear public preferences for one team over the other. There are either few (if any) informed bettors within the WNBA betting market or their presence (or perceived presence) leads the sportsbook to price as a forecast of game outcomes to discourage their participation. In any case, there does not appear to be easy profits to be made for informed traders within this market.

Author Contributions: Rodney J. Paul and Andrew P. Weinbach split the research work on this paper. Andrew P. Weinbach found and gathered the data on the WNBA and did background research on the topic. Rodney J. Paul ran the statistical models, and wrote the manuscript, with insight, editing, and help from his co-author.

Conflicts of Interest: The authors declare no conflict of interest.

References

1. Sportsinsights. Available online: http://www.sportsinsights.com (accessed on 22 April 2014).
2. Humphreys, B.; Paul, R.; Weinbach, A. Consumption Benefits and Gambling: Evidence from the NCAA Basketball Betting Market. *J. Econ. Psychol.* **2013**, *39*, 376–386. [CrossRef]
3. Gramm, M.; Owens, D. Determinants of Betting Market Efficiency. *Appl. Econ. Lett.* **2005**, *12*, 181–185. [CrossRef]

4. Weinbach, A.; Paul, R. The Link between Information and the Favorite-Longshot Bias in Parimutuel Wagering Markets. *J. Gambl. Bus. Econ.* **2008**, *2*, 30–44.
5. Borghesi, R.; Paul, R.; Weinbach, A. Market Frictions and Overpriced Favorites: Evidence from Arena Football. *Appl. Econ. Lett.* **2009**, *16*, 903–906. [CrossRef]
6. Levitt, S. Why are gambling markets organized so differently from financial markets? *Econ. J.* **2004**, *114*, 223–246. [CrossRef]
7. Paul, R.; Weinbach, A. Does Sportsbook.com Set Pointspreads to Maximize Profits? Tests of the Levitt Model of Sportsbook Behavior. *J. Predict. Mark.* **2008**, *1*, 209–218.
8. Paul, R.; Weinbach, A. Price Setting in the NBA Gambling Market: Tests of the Levitt Model of Sportsbook Behavior. *Int. J. Sports Financ.* **2008**, *3*, 2–18.
9. Zuber, R.; Gandar, J.; Bowers, B. Beating the spread: Testing the efficiency of the gambling market for National Football League games. *J. Polit. Econ.* **1985**, *93*, 800–806.
10. Sauer, R. The Economics of Wagering Markets. *J. Econ. Lit.* **1998**, *36*, 2021–2064.
11. Dare, W.; McDonald, S. A Generalized Model for Testing the Home and Favorite Team Advantage in Point Spread Markets. *J. Financ. Econ.* **1996**, *40*, 295–318. [CrossRef]
12. Golec, J.; Tamarkin, M. The degree of inefficiency in the football betting market: Statistical tests. *J. Financ. Econ.* **1991**, *30*, 311–323. [CrossRef]
13. Dare, W.; Holland, S. Efficiency in the NFL Betting Market: Modifying and Consolidating Research Methods. *Appl. Econ.* **2004**, *36*, 9–15. [CrossRef]
14. Gray, P.; Gray, S. Testing market efficiency: Evidence from the NFL sports betting market. *J. Financ.* **1997**, *52*, 1725–1737. [CrossRef]
15. Paul, R.; Weinbach, A. Investigating Allegations of Pointshaving in NCAA Basketball using Actual Sportsbook Percentages. *J. Sports Econ.* **2011**, *12*, 432–447. [CrossRef]
16. Mayer, G. *Bookie: My Life in Disorganized Crime*; J.P. Tarcher, Inc.: Los Angeles, CA, USA, 1974.

International Journal of
Financial Studies

MDPI

Article

"Hot Hand" in the National Basketball Association Point Spread Betting Market: A 34-Year Analysis

Benjamin Waggoner, Daniel Wines, Brian P. Soebbing *, Chad S. Seifried and Jean Michael Martinez

School of Kinesiology, Louisiana State University, Baton Rouge, LA 70803, USA; bwaggo2@lsu.edu (B.W.); dwines2@lsu.edu (D.W.); cseifried@lsu.edu (C.S.S.); jmmartinez@lsu.edu (J.M.M.)
* Author to whom correspondence should be addressed; bsoebb1@lsu.edu; Tel.: +1-225-578-0849.

External Editor: Nicholas Apergis
Received: 4 November 2014; in revised form: 19 November 2014; Accepted: 20 November 2014; Published: 25 November 2014

Abstract: Several articles have looked at factors that affect the adjustments of point spreads, based on hot hands or streaks, for smaller durations of time. This study examines these effects for 34 regular seasons in the National Basketball Association (NBA). Estimating a Seemingly Unrelated Regression model using all 34 seasons, all streaks significantly impacted point spreads and difference in actual points. When estimating each season individually, differences emerged particularly examining winning and losing streaks of six games or more. The results indicate both the presence of momentum effects and the gambler's fallacy.

Keywords: basketball; hot hand; streak; point spread; NBA (National Basketball Association)

1. Introduction

Traditionally, sports betting markets have been compared to simple financial markets, which allowed researchers to examine financial phenomena difficult to observe in other markets [1]. For example, early research regarding sports betting markets focused on the efficiency of these markets (see Sauer [2]) through the rationality between the opening and closing betting lines [3]. Specifically, Sauer's [4] review of the sports betting markets outlined three different types of market efficiency: weak, semi-strong, and strong. Within these forms of market efficiency, numerous other studies looked at biases such as the favorite/longshot bias [5–8], reverse favorite/longshot bias [5,9,10], racial bias [11], and sentiment bias [12–16].

The present research focuses on the team momentum (sometimes called the "hot hand" effect), which received considerable attention in the literature both from psychological [17] and financial [18] perspectives. Paton and Vaughan Williams [19] defined the hot hand as "[. . .] a tendency by bettors to overestimate the extent to which a team or individual's performance is positively autocorrelated" (p. 140). Generally, the literature examining the hot hand effect in betting markets focused on team's winning and losing streaks that occur throughout the regular season. When it comes to betting on the National Basketball Association (NBA), research suggests bettors tend to favor and over bet teams on winning streaks [7,20–23]. In addition, known as betting on the "hot hand", Arkes [18] found evidence showing gamblers overstate the importance of streaks and how it affects the next game's outcome. This belief of streaks is also more commonly known as the gambler's fallacy [24] (p. 1370). Within, it should be noted the over betting on winning streaks can adjust lines and eliminate possible opportunities for truly informed bettors to make a profit [7,22].

One problem with the existing research on the hot hand is the small sample period; thus it may lack generalizability and the data necessary to convince bettors and bookmakers it is indeed a fallacy. As an example, Camerer [20] collected data only from the 1983–1986 seasons, Paul and Weinbach [7] from 1995–2001, Paul and Weinbach [23] from 2004–2006, and Paul and Weinbach [25] from the 2008–2009 season. As Osborne [26] implied, previous research has not considered a long enough time frame to determine if inefficiencies exist in betting markets. In other words, while short-term effects are seen, it is unclear whether these effects persist in the long-term.

Another problem found in the current literature is that there was not much research examining losing streaks. Paul and Weinbach [7] noted, this lack of research could be due to the fact gamblers were more apt to follow teams on winning streaks *versus versus* losing streaks. However, a closer examination of losing streaks could reveal potential profitable betting strategies for bookmakers and bettors over time. While it is important to further current research in betting on favorites, it is just as interesting to analyze teams on losing streaks.

The purpose of the present research is to look at the impact that winning and losing streaks have in NBA point spread betting markets. The time period under examination is the 1979–1980 season through the 2012–2013 season. Covering more than 37,000 games during the sample period, results from a Seemingly Unrelated Regression model to examine point spreads and the actual difference in points scored during the contest indicate momentum effects do exist. However, significant variation is seen from season to season in terms of these momentum effects.

2. Literature Review

While the hot hand effect and potential bias has been a popular area of research in sports betting markets, it has been examined in other contexts as well. Seminal work by Gilovich, Vallone, and Tversky [27] illustrated individuals believed a basketball player would be more likely to make a free throw after making two or three free throws in a row prior to the attempt. Since their study, many other studies have similarly looked at the hot hand belief. [1] Additional research by MacMahon, Köppen, and Raab [29] provided some context as to the reason why people may believe in hot hand effects. They outlined two reasons for the hot hand. The first reason is evolutionary where individuals can identify hot and cold streaks over time and rationalize them. The second reason is exposure based upon Tversky and Kahneman's [30] representativeness heuristic where people misinterpret the actions in front of them as generalized truths. Nickerson [31] stated individuals do not fully comprehend the role of randomness in sports outcomes.

In sports betting markets, previous research examining the hot hand based on winning and losing can also be classified as momentum effects [18]. Camerer [20] sought to understand whether NBA betting markets take into account streaks by measuring the profitability of placing a bet on teams on winning and losing streaks. Examining three seasons of NBA betting odds, he found evidence of momentum effects existing in betting markets but not in actual game outcomes. This finding, he observed, was evidence of the hot hand. However, individuals betting on teams on winning or losing streaks could not make a profit. Interestingly, Brown and Sauer [21], questioned Camerer's [20] original premise of the hot hand being a misrepresentation of randomness when they examined winning and losing streaks of two or three games and four and more games. Within, Brown and Sauer [21] argued Camerer's [20] results reflected a mythical hot hand and did not examine whether observable changes in both point spreads and actual game outcomes were a function of a hot hand. Brown and Sauer [21] found support for Camerer's [20] hypothesis but did not find any support for an actual hot hand. Gray and Gray [32] similarly analyzed the role that NFL team's winning and losing streaks have in betting outcomes (*i.e.*, covering the spread) from 1976 through 1994. Their results found the point spread market during this time period reacted more quickly to recent performance of the NFL teams, but was slow in reacting to the winning and losing streaks of teams over the course of the season.

Paul and Weinbach [7] discovered in their analysis of point spreads 1995–1996 through 2001–2002 the existence of the hot hand effect where bettors over bet teams on winning streaks. However, they

---

[1]   See Bar-eli, Avugos, and Raab [28] and Avugos *et al.* [17] for a recent review of this literature regarding the hot hand effect.

did not find that bettors tended to over bet teams on losing streaks. Paul and Weinbach [7] attributed this difference to a gambler's lower utility with betting on losing teams. Examining the NBA totals market, which is a bet on the combined final point total for the two teams playing in the game, during the same time period, Paul and Weinbach [7] found the hot hand belief did not affect betting behavior.

Paul, Weinbach, and Wilson [22] also found that using streaks to create betting strategies of either betting with the streak or against the streak is not profitable. The only case where the fair bet was violated involved betting the under in games where both teams are coming into play on two or more game under streaks. In addition, they tested strategies of betting with or against streaks under the hot hand hypothesis and no profitability was found. These findings were similar to the results found for totals in professional football, baseball, and hockey. In all cases, the null of a fair bet could be rejected for the largest favorites or largest totals as underdogs won significantly more than 50% of the time. The authors suggested the size of the basketball market is not large enough for uninformed bettors to dominate informed bettors. Therefore, the totals market for the NBA was found to violate a fair bet, but not profitability.

Paul, Weinbach, and Humphreys [33] further looked at the role the hot hand effect plays in betting volume of NBA games over a period from 2003–2004 season through the 2008–2009 season. Their hypothesis was bettors influenced by the hot hand effect would bet more for teams that are winning streaks compared to losing streaks. Results from their research supported this hypothesis. Specifically, they found away teams on winning streaks of two games generated a higher percentage of bets compared to home teams on winning streaks. Home teams on winning streaks of four games or more generated a higher proportion of bets (2.2%) compared to away teams on similar streaks (1.9%).

Other recent research by Arkes [18] examined team momentum in NBA betting markets, which was defined by winning and losing streaks but also the strength of game outcomes. Examining a longer sample of NBA regular season games, Arkes [18] concluded hot hand effects were real. Despite gamblers being correct that a hot hand effect exists, there was evidence showing gamblers overstated the importance of streaks and their effect on the streaking team's next game's outcome [18].

In summary, a rich literature has been developed toward examining team momentum in all different contexts. Within sport betting markets, momentum effects present evidence that bettors believe in a mythical hot hand effect. However, there are conflicting findings showing whether or not the hot hand is real. One limitation of the previous research is the short sample periods to look at this effect. As Osborne [26] remarked, previous studies looking at inefficiencies in the sports betting markets do not examine a long enough time horizon. Thus, momentum effects such as the winning and losing streak of teams may persist in the short-term but not necessarily in the long-term. The present research investigates this effect over a longer time period.

3. Methods

To examine the hot hand in the NBA, the sample period looks at regular season point spreads and game outcomes from the 1979–1980 season through the end of the 2012–2013 season. NBA regular season game data from multiple websites including Basketball Reference and NBA.com were retrieved. Information regarding the point spread data for these games was collected from both online websites as well as newspapers. In total, there were 37,179 individual games over this period of time. Over the time period, there were 17 games in which point spreads were not located when using various sources such as websites and newspaper articles. Thus, the final data set includes 37,162 NBA games during the sample period.

In the present research, the following model is estimated:

$$DV_{hags} = \alpha_{DV} + A_{hgs} + A_{ags} + STRK_{hgs} + STRK_{ags} + \varepsilon_{hags} \tag{1}$$

where h indexes home teams, a indexes away teams, g indexes games and s indexes seasons, and ε is the equation error term. There are two dependent variables in the present research. The first is the point spread for the game in relation to the home team (*PS*). The second dependent variable is the difference in the final score between the home team and the away team (*DP*). A_{hgs} is a parameter examining the home ability index for team h in game g in season s. A_{ags} is the visiting ability index for team a in game g in season s.[2] ε is the equation error term. The main variables of interest are the streaks for the home ($STRK_{hgs}$)) and away ($STRK_{ags}$)) teams prior to the observed game. In the present research, these streak variables look at winning and losing streaks of two, four, and six or more games. For example, the variable *VL2* takes the value of 1 if the away team is on a losing streak of two or three games going into the observed game. As a result, there are 12 indicator variables.

Table 1 presents the summary statistics for the variables in the present research. It shows the average point spread is −3.77 meaning the home team is favored by 3.77 points which reflects the home court advantage in the NBA. The average difference in points is −3.71 meaning the home team won by an average of 3.71 points during the sample period. *Error* is the difference between the point spread and the actual difference in points showing that the spread favors the home team by about 0.06 of a point compared to the actual final difference in points. This reflects the accuracy of the bookmakers in predicting the final outcome of the match.

Table 1. Summary Statistics (n = 37,162).

Variable	Description	Mean	Std. Dev.	Min	Max
PS	Closing point spread in observed game	−3.775	6.208	−25	49
DP	Actual difference in points in observed game (visiting team–home team)	−3.714	12.885	−68	56
Error	Difference between the closing point spread and difference in points	0.061	11.398	−61.5	62.5
VL2	Visiting team has a losing streak of 2 or 3 games	0.215	0.411	0	1
VL4	Visiting team has a losing streak of 3 or 4 games	0.065	0.246	0	1
VL6	Visiting team has a losing streak of 6 or more games	0.045	0.208	0	1
VW2	Visiting team has a winning streak of 2 or 3 games	0.136	0.343	0	1
VW4	Visiting team has a winning streak of 3 or 4 games	0.046	0.208	0	1
VW6	Visiting team has a winning streak of 6 or more games	0.031	0.174	0	1
HL2	Home team has a losing streak of 2 or 3 games	0.131	0.338	0	1
HL4	Home team has a losing streak of 3 or 4 games	0.045	0.208	0	1
HL6	Home team has a losing streak of 6 or more games	0.036	0.186	0	1
HW2	Visiting team has a winning streak of 2 or 3 games	0.221	0.415	0	1
HW4	Home team has a winning streak of 3 or 4 games	0.066	0.248	0	1
HW6	Home team has a winning streak of 6 or more games	0.044	0.205	0	1

The main variables of interest are the 12 streak variables. A visiting team with a losing streak of two or three games occurred in more than 21 percent of the sample. Similar percentages were found for a two or three game home winning streak. The smallest streak that occurred in the sample was a home team on a losing streak of six or more games (3.6% of the sample observations).

Consistent with Brown and Sauer's [21] research, the present research estimates a Seemingly Unrelated Regression (SUR) to analyze the relationship between the point spreads and the actual game outcomes. We use generalized least squares in the SUR technique to control for the heteroscedasticity of both error terms [34]. As Arkes [18] explained, "[t]he justification [for using SUR] is that the error terms for both models would include factors known to the odds makers and gamblers, but not observable or quantifiable to the Researcher" (p. 36). These factors could include the game's referee assignments and knowledge of injuries to players. Similar to Brown and Sauer [21], all the seasons are pooled into one model. Thus, there are home and away abilities for each team for each season to control for the changing abilities of teams from year to year.

---

2   The ability indexes for the home and visiting team are measured using home and visiting team fixed effects.

Int. J. Financial Stud. **2014**, *2*, 359–370

4. Results and Discussion

Table 2 presents the SUR results. The "R^2" reported in both models is consistent with previous research where Equation 1 explains more of the observed variation in the point spreads than in the actual difference in points. Looking at Table 2, significant results are found for all but one of the streak variables' coefficients. Only the coefficient for the variable indicating the visiting team is on a winning streak of two or three games is insignificant. This result could be that bettors do not perceive visiting teams on a small winning streak to be "hot".

Table 2. Seemingly Unrelated Regression (SUR) Regression Results: Pooled Model.

Dep. Var.	Point Spread			Difference in Points		
Variable	Coef.	Stnd.Error	*p*-value	Coef.	Stnd.Error	*p*-value
VL2	−0.176	0.035	<0.001	−4.320	0.129	<0.001
VL4	−0.646	0.056	<0.001	−4.408	0.206	<0.001
VL6	−1.182	0.069	<0.001	−4.583	0.252	<0.001
VW2	0.032	0.043	0.458	7.574	0.157	<0.001
VW4	0.435	0.066	<0.001	7.288	0.241	<0.001
VW6	0.727	0.080	<0.001	7.203	0.292	<0.001
HL2	0.121	0.043	0.005	7.608	0.159	<0.001
HL4	0.683	0.066	<0.001	7.601	0.243	<0.001
HL6	1.463	0.076	<0.001	7.651	0.280	<0.001
HW2	−0.130	0.035	<0.001	−4.401	0.128	<0.001
HW4	−0.398	0.055	<0.001	−4.148	0.202	<0.001
HW6	−0.745	0.068	<0.001	−4.402	0.250	<0.001
"R2"	0.8472			0.5236		

Looking specifically at the other eleven significant coefficients, the signs on the coefficients are expected based upon previous research. For example, the coefficient on the variable where the visiting team is on a losing streak of two or three games decreases the point spread by 0.176 points meaning the home team is more favored in the match. Overall, the results presented in Table 2 are consistent with Arkes' [18] findings and the belief in momentum effects showing up in point spreads. The results provided within this paper also confirm belief in the hot hand within betting markets as shown in earlier research such as Camerer [20], Brown and Sauer [21] and Paul and Weinbach [7]. Thus, when a home team is on a losing streak, the point spread will react by increasing, meaning that the home team is becoming more of an underdog.

It is also observed that streaks of six or more games whether on winning or losing or home or away, showed a greater influence on the point spread than teams on streaks of four or more. This observation may be attributed to the gambler's fallacy [24]. Streaks of two or three games occur frequently throughout the season of the NBA. When a team is on a losing streak of four or five games, bettors may believe that the team will win (lose) soon because they are "due" for a win (loss) since they have lost (won) several games in a row, thus committing the gambler's fallacy. However, when these streaks continue on and become streaks of six or more games, bettors may be more likely to contribute this scenario to the team being legitimately good if they are on a winning streak or legitimately bad if they are on a losing streak.

Examining the results with the dependent variable being the difference in actual points scored, all of the streak variables' coefficients are significant with the expected signs. Recall a negative difference in points means that the home team scores more points than the away team. In Table 2, a visiting team on a losing streak of two or three games decreases the difference in points by 4.3. Looking at the magnitude of the coefficients, visiting team winning streaks and home team losing streaks have a higher impact in terms of the difference in points compared to visiting team losing streak and home team winning streaks. These results are inconsistent with Brown and Sauer's [21] findings. In their research, they found streaks did not have any effect on actual game outcomes.

Alternative Estimation

While the pooled model looks at the impact of the hot hand effect over the course of the 34-year period, significant variation could exist between seasons in examining the hot hand effects. Thus, we estimated Equation 1 for each individual season, consistent with Soebbing and Humphreys' [34] approach for examining the perception of tanking in NBA betting markets. Table 3 presents the findings for the point spread portion of the SUR model while Table 4 provides the difference in points. The coefficients in bold on both tables are significant at the 1 percent level while the last column and last row on both tables reflect the totals for the row/column. In looking at Table 3, there are approximately three significant streak parameters per year. The largest streaks (*HL6, HW6, VL6, VW6*) are the highest frequency in terms of the significance at the 1 percent level. This finding is evidence of the mythical hot hand or team momentum effects since point spreads adjust the most for winning and losing streaks of six or more games. Examining Table 4, there are almost 11 significant streak parameters per season when looking at the difference in points. In contrast to Table 3 where the largest streaks had the highest frequency in terms of significance, they tend to have the lowest frequency in terms of significance for the actual difference in points. While there cannot be any definitive conclusions, it would seem to indicate the presence of an occurrence where bettors tend to perceive that long streaks will continue and bookmakers account for this perception. In actuality, however, there is no indication that large streaks affect the actual difference in points.

Overall, the results presented in Table 4 shows team momentum do consistently impact actual game outcomes throughout the same period. There is no indication that gambling behavior changes systematically from one year to the next year. When examining changes in the NBA, however, there are several reasons why this result may occur. The first reason is changes in the NBA's amateur draft, the mechanism in which amateur players are allocated to professional clubs, to deter teams to intentionally lose late in the regular season to earn a higher probability of selecting first overall in the amateur draft [34]. Thus, the significant coefficients on the winning and losing streak variables may reflect this behavior that has been found in previous research to occur throughout this time period (see Soebbing and Humphreys for a review of this literature [34]). The second reason is due to additional fundamental factors that may impact the point spread and actual game outcomes. Research by Brown and Sauer [35] found evidence that point spreads are impacted by fundamental factors rather than just irrelevant noise. The significant coefficients in both Tables 3 and 4 may also reflect some of these fundamental factors.

Table 3. Season SUR Results: Point Spread.

Season/Streak	VL2	VL4	VL6	VW2	VW4	VW6	HL2	HL4	HL6	HW2	HW4	HW6	Total
1979	0.16	−0.26	−0.45	0.16	−0.59	0.38	−0.06	−0.46	**1.23**	0.01	0.28	−0.33	1
1980	0.12	0.02	−0.21	0.04	0.44	**−0.67**	0.02	0.17	0.79	0.25	0.31	−0.07	1
1981	−0.16	**−1.18**	**−1.84**	0.10	0.07	0.53	0.11	−0.01	**2.53**	0.07	−0.30	−0.62	3
1982	−0.26	−0.54	**−1.49**	0.46	**1.45**	0.97	−0.37	−0.35	0.64	−0.12	−0.01	−0.81	2
1983	−0.29	−0.82	−1.36	−0.10	0.29	0.13	−0.21	−0.29	−0.03	−0.21	**−1.14**	−1.03	1
1984	−0.28	−0.27	**−2.16**	0.00	**1.20**	**1.43**	−0.03	**1.46**	**2.30**	0.01	−0.11	**−1.04**	6
1985	−0.09	−0.27	−0.95	−0.41	0.25	0.38	0.08	**1.13**	1.12	−0.24	−0.35	−0.43	1
1986	0.16	−0.54	−0.86	−0.15	−0.04	0.25	0.27	−0.40	0.82	−0.15	−0.61	−0.58	0
1987	−0.05	0.10	0.36	−0.18	−0.10	0.79	0.28	0.59	0.65	−0.40	−0.05	−1.16	1
1988	0.06	−0.40	**−1.76**	0.07	0.02	0.62	0.03	−0.18	1.06	−0.25	−0.75	−0.97	1
1989	−0.09	−0.67	**−0.92**	−0.13	**1.16**	0.98	0.41	0.71	**1.25**	**−0.51**	−0.34	**−0.90**	5
1990	−0.11	−0.62	**−1.08**	0.09	0.24	0.63	−0.06	0.93	0.76	−0.18	−0.30	−0.28	1
1991	−0.10	**−1.38**	**−1.80**	−0.12	0.76	1.14	0.21	**1.19**	**1.77**	−0.10	−0.29	−1.15	4
1992	−0.34	−0.82	−0.97	−0.34	−0.08	**1.33**	0.28	0.78	**1.28**	−0.09	**−1.08**	**−1.45**	4
1993	−0.42	−0.55	**−1.36**	0.22	**1.24**	0.07	0.07	0.33	**1.08**	−0.28	−0.39	**−0.78**	4
1994	0.04	−0.18	−0.75	0.16	0.51	**1.24**	−0.08	0.21	0.43	−0.07	−0.38	−0.99	1
1995	−0.11	−0.59	−0.64	−0.18	0.65	**1.46**	−0.05	0.60	0.99	−0.32	−0.65	**−1.24**	2
1996	−0.11	−0.40	−0.60	−0.06	0.48	0.91	0.45	0.51	**1.79**	−0.53	−0.50	−0.44	1
1997	−0.27	−0.39	−0.79	−0.28	0.41	**1.38**	0.15	0.59	**1.20**	−0.25	**−0.80**	−0.48	3
1998	−0.26	−0.10	−0.44	−0.67	−0.32	0.93	0.27	**1.43**	0.80	−0.15	−0.66	−0.16	1
1999	−0.04	−0.41	**−1.42**	0.08	0.47	**1.41**	−0.27	0.60	**2.00**	−0.05	−0.50	−0.02	3
2000	−0.21	−0.39	−0.83	0.23	0.42	0.50	0.12	0.31	**1.35**	−0.19	−0.44	−1.00	1
2001	−0.17	**−1.45**	−0.97	0.04	0.32	0.51	0.23	1.06	**1.64**	−0.42	−0.02	−0.61	2
2002	−0.14	−0.77	**−1.34**	0.25	0.67	0.58	0.00	0.59	0.60	0.10	−0.15	−0.54	1
2003	−0.21	−0.71	**−1.12**	0.20	**1.39**	**1.89**	0.05	0.31	**2.58**	0.12	−0.42	**−1.67**	5
2004	−0.37	**−0.99**	**−1.28**	0.14	**1.86**	**1.54**	0.43	**1.36**	**2.32**	−0.22	−0.75	**−1.52**	7
2005	−0.47	**−1.00**	**−2.40**	0.30	0.86	0.64	0.03	**1.11**	**1.31**	0.09	**−0.92**	−1.05	5
2006	**−0.61**	**−1.75**	**−1.76**	0.12	0.51	0.73	0.27	0.99	**2.71**	−0.07	**−0.88**	−0.85	5
2007	**−0.75**	−0.86	−1.17	−0.11	0.30	0.47	0.12	**1.51**	1.16	−0.19	−0.38	−0.89	2
2008	0.35	−0.16	−1.09	0.08	0.25	1.06	−0.11	0.89	1.05	−0.33	−0.70	**−1.56**	1
2009	0.22	−0.17	**−1.29**	0.04	0.73	**1.56**	**0.71**	0.85	**1.79**	−0.08	−0.51	−0.93	4
2010	−0.22	−0.53	**−1.12**	0.42	−0.14	1.01	0.12	**1.39**	**1.76**	0.22	−0.24	−0.71	3
2011	−0.38	−0.95	**−1.94**	−0.01	0.28	0.61	0.02	1.03	**2.51**	0.02	−0.01	**−3.10**	3
2012	−0.21	−0.56	**−1.15**	0.14	−0.03	0.57	0.14	0.53	**2.33**	−0.11	−0.34	−0.47	2
Total	2	6	19	0	6	10	1	8	20	1	5	10	

Int. J. Financial Stud. **2014**, *2*, 359–370

Table 4. Season SUR Results: Difference in Points.

Season/Streak	VL2	VL4	VL6	VW2	VW4	VW6	HL2	HL4	HL6	HW2	HW4	HW6	Total
1979	−4.18	−3.37	−5.46	7.68	1.26	4.77	8.15	7.33	7.66	−4.02	−3.00	−4.07	7
1980	−2.67	−2.34	−3.17	8.84	−0.71	8.98	7.36	4.53	8.01	−4.31	−1.04	−1.87	7
1981	−2.68	−3.14	−3.08	8.02	6.74	7.77	7.69	6.92	6.16	−3.46	−3.85	−2.84	9
1982	−4.34	−5.10	−4.11	7.52	4.96	7.92	6.34	7.98	8.13	−5.33	−3.87	−7.36	12
1983	−2.10	−2.59	−3.06	8.09	8.45	5.99	9.10	7.86	8.96	−4.22	−3.77	−0.71	9
1984	−4.74	−5.52	−4.50	7.49	8.63	6.59	8.11	5.87	8.48	−4.64	−3.51	−4.15	11
1985	−4.83	−4.88	−3.55	8.28	5.90	7.71	7.69	9.29	6.05	−4.12	−3.55	−3.16	10
1986	−3.18	−2.41	−3.04	9.33	7.15	5.88	8.91	10.58	10.13	−3.53	−2.22	−4.32	6
1987	−3.29	−4.17	−3.60	7.51	7.04	9.73	8.75	7.69	10.33	−3.26	−3.48	−3.70	11
1988	−3.72	−3.84	−3.83	8.68	9.03	8.69	7.87	6.20	8.33	−3.34	−4.29	−3.58	11
1989	−4.15	−5.29	−5.07	7.80	7.47	7.66	8.87	8.34	6.61	−3.35	−4.24	−7.64	12
1990	−4.02	−4.76	−2.75	9.42	7.21	10.42	8.09	7.12	11.60	−2.95	−2.82	−4.04	10
1991	−5.04	−3.71	−4.11	7.27	7.62	5.24	6.82	6.55	8.84	−4.24	−5.24	−5.46	12
1992	−4.44	−4.17	−5.98	6.42	6.86	9.42	9.33	9.12	8.95	−5.00	−6.39	−5.13	12
1993	−3.91	−5.68	−4.07	7.80	5.38	6.72	7.49	8.25	7.55	−4.49	−3.96	−3.68	12
1994	−5.18	−4.08	−2.19	7.92	8.30	7.23	7.38	7.13	7.17	−4.68	−5.65	−5.37	11
1995	−4.68	−3.66	−5.54	7.34	8.45	7.69	8.59	5.25	7.41	−3.08	−4.76	−3.65	11
1996	−5.97	−6.52	−5.74	7.21	9.98	9.82	5.44	6.32	5.45	−4.60	−2.85	−4.51	11
1997	−4.47	−5.13	−3.22	7.33	7.02	8.55	7.15	8.47	6.60	−4.22	−3.59	−4.16	12
1998	−4.87	−4.63	−4.04	7.71	6.95	9.17	7.02	8.26	3.49	−3.56	−2.50	−6.32	9
1999	−3.92	−2.09	−5.10	7.82	7.61	8.40	6.86	8.02	7.29	−4.44	−4.51	−2.09	10
2000	−4.91	−6.36	−6.56	7.25	8.68	5.91	6.61	4.72	8.31	−4.69	−5.42	−4.60	12
2001	−4.21	−5.52	−6.34	7.58	9.21	7.48	5.58	7.02	7.27	−5.23	−4.88	−6.97	12
2002	−4.74	−3.36	−5.30	7.73	7.57	6.93	7.74	6.43	4.77	−4.94	−5.12	−6.87	12
2003	−3.50	−4.45	−4.93	6.40	6.87	8.91	8.15	10.00	8.04	−4.42	−5.25	−5.79	12
2004	−5.12	−4.14	−4.39	6.72	9.34	6.26	6.67	7.38	5.72	−4.76	−4.46	−7.01	12
2005	−4.01	−3.24	−5.16	8.07	8.81	8.39	7.55	7.26	8.87	−4.09	−5.87	−4.56	12
2006	−5.41	−5.65	−2.33	6.68	8.49	7.16	7.70	8.48	8.61	−5.20	−4.21	−3.95	11
2007	−3.62	−2.79	−4.26	7.96	8.35	9.43	6.29	10.40	7.34	−5.66	−6.19	−5.45	11
2008	−3.68	−5.28	−5.55	7.67	6.34	7.69	8.06	7.17	8.71	−4.47	−5.83	−5.98	12
2009	−5.06	−5.62	−6.88	8.87	8.12	7.52	7.30	7.00	7.02	−5.49	−3.13	−5.19	12
2010	−4.68	−3.51	−5.75	6.65	6.96	8.55	7.93	7.69	6.23	−5.05	−4.84	−3.12	11
2011	−5.54	−5.11	−5.79	6.60	8.29	6.78	8.60	8.40	8.90	−4.57	−4.47	−9.99	12
2012	−4.78	−6.20	−4.61	7.64	7.60	8.41	8.21	8.18	7.11	−5.10	−3.01	−2.56	11
Total	32	26	24	34	32	32	34	34	33	34	28	22	

5. Conclusions

The theory of the "hot hand" has been a topic studied by several researchers in different fields. Within sports betting markets, team momentum effects are a popular area of analysis with particular emphasis looking at NBA games. While previous research indicates that point spreads are adjusted based upon winning and losing streaks indicating the myth of the hot hand occurs, the research is mixed in terms of how winning and losing streaks affect actual games outcomes, which would signify an actual hot hand. However, previous research examined only short sample periods. The present research looked at a 34-year period of NBA regular season point spreads and actual games outcomes. A pooled sample found streaks impacted both point spreads and actual games outcomes. Furthermore, estimating each year individually found significant variation in how streaks impact point spreads and actual games outcomes. In particular, it was found that large winning and losing streaks imposed the most effect on point spreads but not on actual game outcomes.

Overall the findings looking at the hot hand effect measured by streaks in the present research are consistent with Arkes' [18] findings in a larger study of NBA regular season games. Furthermore, Arkes [18] concluded that momentum effects do exist and are not mythical. The results in Table 2 would suggest that momentum effects are indeed real and they affect both the point spreads set by bookmakers and the actual difference in points scored by the two teams.

Finally, although this research is not examining a strategy of betting on the streaks, it does provide information that future research could use to look at long-term betting strategies. As recent research provides increasing information that bookmakers are profit maximizers instead of balancing the dollar

Int. J. Financial Stud. **2014**, *2*, 359–370

values between the favorites and underdogs of a particular match (e.g., [23,36,37]), future research could look at how book makers use betting beliefs regarding the hot hand to maximize profits. Recent research by Paul *et al.* [33] began to analyze this phenomenon using five years of betting volume data. An additional area of future research would be the analysis of how the point spread changes from the opening line to closing line to see how accurately the original point spread was set. The movement of the point spread would also reflect the placement of bets that would occur on a game.

Acknowledgments: We would like to thank Andy Weinbach and Richard Gandar for their assistance in obtaining many of the earlier point spreads used in this manuscript and Josh Pratt for his helpful research assistance.

Author Contributions: Benjamin Waggoner and Daniel Wines constructed the streak variables, collected 5 seasons of NBA point spreads and provided the initial statistical analysis. Brian P. Soebbing merged the data together and conducted the final statistical analysis. Soebbing along with Chad S. Seifried and Jean Michael Martinez wrote the final manuscript.

Conflicts of Interest: The authors declare no conflict of interest.

References

1. Gandar, J.M.; Dare, W.H.; Brown, C.R.; Zuber, R.A. Informed traders and price variations in the betting market for professional basketball games. *J. Financ.* **1998**, *53*, 385–401. [CrossRef]
2. Sauer, R.D. The state of research on markets for sports betting and suggested future directions. *J. Econ. Financ.* **2005**, *29*, 416–426. [CrossRef]
3. Gandar, J.M.; Zuber, R.A.; O'Brien, T.; Russo, B. Testing rationality in the point spread betting market. *J. Financ.* **1998**, *43*, 995–1008. [CrossRef]
4. Sauer, R.D. The economics of wagering markets. *J. Econ. Lit.* **1998**, *36*, 2021–2064.
5. Gandar, J.M.; Zuber, R.A.; Johnson, R.S.; Dare, W. Re-examining the betting market on Major League Baseball games: Is there a reverse favourite-longshot bias? *Appl. Econ.* **2002**, *34*, 1307–1317. [CrossRef]
6. Golic, J.; Tamarkin, M. The degree of inefficiency in the football betting market. *J. Financ. Econ.* **1991**, *30*, 311–323. [CrossRef]
7. Paul, R.J.; Weinbach, A.P. Bettor misconceptions in the NBA: The overbetting of large favorites and the "hot hand". *J. Sport. Econ.* **2005**, *6*, 390–400. [CrossRef]
8. Williams, L.V.; Paton, D. Why are some favourite-longshot biases positive and others negative? *Appl. Econ.* **1998**, *30*, 1505–1510. [CrossRef]
9. Woodland, L.M.; Woodland, B.M. The reverse favourite-longshot bias and market efficiency in Major League Baseball: An update. *Bull. Econ. Res.* **2003**, *55*, 113–123. [CrossRef]
10. Woodland, L.M.; Woodland, B.M. Market efficiency and the favourite-longshot bias: The baseball betting market. *J. Financ.* **1994**, *49*, 269–279. [CrossRef]
11. Larsen, T.; Price, J.; Wolfers, J. Racial bias in the NBA: Implications for betting markets. *J. Quant. Anal. Sport.* **2008**, *4*. Article 7.
12. Avery, C.; Chevalier, J. Identifying investor sentiment from price paths: The case of football betting. *J. Bus.* **1999**, *72*, 493–521. [CrossRef]
13. Bernile, G.; Lyandres, E. Understanding investor sentiment: The case of soccer. *Financ. Manag.* **2011**, *40*, 357–380. [CrossRef]
14. Braun, S.; Kvansnicka, M. National sentiment and economic behavior: Evidence from online betting on European football. *J. Sport. Econ.* **2013**, *14*, 45–64. [CrossRef]
15. Feddersen, A.; Humphreys, B.R.; Soebbing, B.P. Sentiment bias in National Basketball Association Betting. Available online: http://www.be.wvu.edu/phd_economics/pdf/13-03.pdf (accessed on 14 April 2014).
16. Forrest, D.; Simmons, R. Sentiment in the betting market of Spanish football. *Appl. Econ.* **2008**, *40*, 119–126. [CrossRef]
17. Avugos, S.; Köppen, J.; Czienskowski, U.; Raab, M.; Bar-Eli, M. The "hot hand" reconsidered: A meta-analytic approach. *Psychol. Sport. Exerc.* **2013**, *14*, 21–27. [CrossRef]
18. Arkes, J. Do gamblers correctly price momentum in NBA betting markets? *J. Predict. Mark* **2011**, *5*, 30–52.
19. Paton, D.; Vaughan Williams, L. Forecasting outcomes in spread betting markets: Can bettors use 'Quarbs' to beat the book? *J. Forecast.* **2005**, *24*, 139–154. [CrossRef]

20. Camerer, C.F. Does the basketball market believe in the "hot hand"? *Am. Econ. Rev.* **1989**, *79*, 1257–1261.
21. Brown, W.O.; Sauer, R.D. Does the basketball market believe in the 'hot hand'? *Am. Econ. Rev.* **1993**, *83*, 1377–1386.
22. Paul, R.J.; Weinbach, A.P.; Wilson, M. Efficient markets, fair bets, and profitability in NBA totals 1995–96 to 2001–02. *Q. Rev. Econ. Financ.* **2004**, *44*, 624–632. [CrossRef]
23. Paul, R.J.; Weinbach, A.P. Price setting in the NBA gambling market: Tests of the Levitt model of Sportsbook behavior. *Int. J. Sport Financ.* **2008**, *3*, 137–145.
24. Ayton, P.; Fischer, I. The hot hand fallacy and the gambler's fallacy: Two faces of subjective randomness? *Mem. Cogn.* **2004**, *32*, 1369–1378. [CrossRef]
25. Paul, R.J.; Weinbach, A.P. The determinants of betting volume for sports in North America: Evidence of sports betting as consumption in the NBA and NHL. *Int. J. Sport Financ.* **2010**, *5*, 128–140.
26. Osborne, E. Efficient markets? Don't bet on it. *J. Sport. Econ.* **2001**, *2*, 50–61. [CrossRef]
27. Gilovich, T.; Vallone, R.; Tversky, A. The hot hand in basketball: On the misperception of random sequences. *Cogn. Psychol.* **1985**, *17*, 295–314. [CrossRef]
28. Bar-Eli, M.; Avugos, S.; Raab, M. Twenty years of "hot hand" research: Review and critique. *Psychol. Sport Exerc.* **2006**, *7*, 525–553. [CrossRef]
29. MacMahon, C.; Köppen, J.; Raab, M. The hot hand belief and framing effects. *Res. Quart. Exerc. Sport.* **2014**, *85*, 341–350. [CrossRef]
30. Tversky, A.; Kahneman, D. Belief in the law of small numbers. *Psychol. Bull.* **1971**, *76*, 105–110. [CrossRef]
31. Nickerson, R.S. The production and perception of randomness. *Psychol. Rev.* **2002**, *109*, 330–357. [CrossRef] [PubMed]
32. Gray, P.K.; Gray, S.F. Testing market efficiency: Evidence from the NFL sports betting market. *J. Financ.* **1997**, *52*, 1725–1737. [CrossRef]
33. Paul, R.J.; Weinbach, A.P.; Humphreys, B. Revisiting the "hot hand" hypothesis in the NBA betting market using actual sportsbook betting percentages on favorites and underdogs. *J. Gambl. Bus. Econ.* **2011**, *5*, 42–56.
34. Soebbing, B.P.; Humphreys, B.R. Do gamblers think that teams tank? Evidence from the NBA. *Contemp. Econ. Policy* **2013**, *31*, 301–313. [CrossRef]
35. Brown, W.O.; Sauer, R.D. Fundamentals or Noise? Evidence from the professional basketball betting market. *J. Financ.* **1993**, *48*, 1193–1209. [CrossRef]
36. Humphreys, B.R. Point spread shading and behavioral biases in NBA betting markets. *Rivista Di Diritto Ed Economia Dello Sport* **2010**, *VI*, 13–26.
37. Levitt, S.D. Why are gambling markets organized so differently from financial markets? *Econ. J.* **2004**, *114*, 223–245. [CrossRef]

MDPI

St. Alban-Anlage 66

4052 Basel, Switzerland

Tel. +41 61 683 77 34

Fax +41 61 302 89 18

http://www.mdpi.com

International Journal of Financial Studies Editorial Office

E-mail: ijfs@mdpi.com

http://www.mdpi.com/journal/ijfs

www.ingramcontent.com/pod-product-compliance
Lightning Source LLC
Chambersburg PA
CBHW051916210326
41597CB00033B/6163